Hostas

Rosemary Barrett

Photography Derek Hughes

FIREFLY BOOKS

Dedication
For my good friend Bill Robinson
of Rotorua, New Zealand, in
gratitude for his generous sharing of
knowledge, and for an endless supply
of beautiful plants.

Acknowledgements
As usual my thanks go to my valued
editor, Tracey Borgfeldt, and to Derek
Hughes and Anne Bayliss, for without
their diverse skills this book would
not have been possible.

Author's note
The names of hostas in this book
have been spelled according to their
entry in the Naamlijst van Vaste
Planten.

PHOTOGRAPHS

PAGE 1: 'Green Fountain'

PAGE 2: The spectacular 'Patriot' in a
container

PAGE 3: 'Frances Williams'

PAGE 4: 'Great Expectations'

PAGE 5: (from top to bottom) *H. ventricosa;*
'Aurora Borealis'; 'Sunny Smiles'; a
large hosta provides dramatic foliage
in this formal bed; *Kalmia* 'Sarah'
with 'Blue Angel' in the foreground

A FIREFLY BOOK

Published by Firefly Books Ltd. 2004

Originated in 2004 by David Bateman Ltd., 30 Tarndale Grove, Albany,
Auckland, New Zealand

Copyright © 2004 Rosemary Barrett, Derek Hughes and
David Bateman Ltd.

First Printing

Publisher Cataloguing-in-Publication Data (U.S.)

Barrett, Rosemary, 1931-
    Hostas / Rosemary Barrett ; Derek Hughes, photographer. —1st ed.
    [144] p. : col. photos. ;   cm.
    Includes bibliographical references and index.
    Summary: Introductory guide to growing hostas, including hardiness zone
    information. Provides practical advice on how to plant, propagate,
    cultivate and landscape with hostas, including information on companion
    plants.
    ISBN 1-55297-887-7
    ISBN 1-55297-886-9 (pbk.)
    1. Hostas. I. Hughes, Derek. II. Title.
    635.9/3432 21   SB413.H73.B37   2004

National Library of Canada Cataloguing in Publication

Barrett, Rosemary
    Hostas / Rosemary Barrett ; photographs by Derek Hughes.
Includes bibliographical references and index.
ISBN 1-55297-887-7 (bound).—ISBN 1-55297-886-9 (pbk.)
    1. Hosta. I. Hughes, Derek II. Title.
SB413.H73B37 2004   635.93432   C2003-905568-X

Published in the United States in 2004 by
Firefly Books (U.S.) Inc.
P.O. Box 1338, Ellicott Station
Buffalo, New York 14205

Published in Canada in 2004 by
Firefly Books Ltd.
3680 Victoria Park Avenue
Toronto, Ontario M2H 3K1

Printed in China through Colorcraft Ltd., HK

Contents

Introduction

Hostas are plants grown for their wonderful foliage of infinite variation. Depending on the species or cultivar, the hosta can have blue, green, yellow or variegated leaves in a wide variety of shapes, sizes and textures. The plants may be grown separately or mixed with other plants that like the same conditions. Hostas appear in early spring and disappear in late fall, and are hardy to zone 3. The hosta also has the grace to produce a very acceptable flower in colors ranging from white to pale lavenders and blue-purples.

To my mind the hosta is, without a doubt, a perfect perennial. Anyone who wishes to grow it can; no matter how small the garden there is always a place (partly shaded and damp) for at least one or two plants. They also look wonderful grown in containers (and there is always room for one or two of these).

My knowledge comes from years of growing these lovely plants. In this book I would like to share my experience of how, why and where to grow hostas and discuss which hostas, out of the infinite choices available, I have found to be best for the garden. For ease of use, I have listed all the species and varieties mentioned in the book in chapter 9, including details of leaf color and plant size.

There has been a great upsurge in the use of hostas in gardens in the last few years, no doubt because they are not only beautiful, and beautifully diverse, but because they are very easy to grow. For the modern gardener who does not have a great deal of time, or perhaps does not wish to spend it in the garden, the hosta is an answer to a prayer. As we shall see in chapters 2 and 3, their cultivation is easy – and the rewards are great.

While understanding the constraints of budget, it seems a great pity to perhaps own half a dozen of the more common varieties and just keep splitting them up and spreading them around the garden. I feel continuity can be taken too far, and that gardeners are limiting themselves by ignoring the beautiful and different hostas that are available. I hope this book will provide you with information on not only what is available but the many ways in which these lovely plants can be used and enjoyed.

PREVIOUS PAGES: A mixed hosta planting covering a large partly shaded bank.
OPPOSITE: An exuberant woodland garden in full flower.

Discovery and Development

European introduction

Most hosta species hail from Japan, where they were known as early as the 8th century. Because of this, I had always thought that the first introduction of hostas into Europe came from that country. But not so, the first hostas came from seeds sent from China that were then planted in the Jardin des Plantes in Paris, France. This hosta was *Hosta plantaginea*, and it is still widely grown today. Then a wealthy Englishman imported both *H. plantaginea* and another species, *H. ventricosa* (also still grown today), and grew them under glass. It soon became apparent that they were actually suited to the temperate British climate and so they were grown outside. These two species remained the only hostas grown in European gardens until 1829.

In the early 17th century Japan opened its borders, which had previously been closed to foreigners. This generosity was to last only 30 years. Missionaries, many from Catholic Portugal, upset the Japanese authorities, and they promptly shut their borders to all Westerners except the Protestant Dutch. The Dutch were more interested in developing trade than spreading their religious beliefs. Chinese and Korean traders were also granted access. With Japan being closed to Europeans, the only Westerners allowed in were men in the employ of the Dutch East India Company. A settlement was created on an

OPPOSITE: One of the most popular hosta species for the garden, *H. sieboldiana*, and the cultivar 'Fringe Benefit'.

RIGHT: The first hosta in cultivation in the West, *H. plantaginea*.

HOSTA SPECIES

TOP: The lush green and white leaves of *H. undulata*, with the dark green *H. sieboldiana* in the background.

ABOVE: H. montana

I had always thought that any plant found growing in the wild was a species. I also thought that if a cultivar came true from seed that it must be a species. Not so. A plant can grow in the wild all it likes, but until botanists get hold of it, thoroughly research it and publish a botanical name, it is not a legitimate species. All this must be fun for botanists, and there are of course differences of opinion among many of them as to what constitutes a species. This study is important to botanists and horticulturists, but to gardeners it is rather academic. We grow what we know and like, and are not too concerned about whether a hosta is a species, a cultivar or something called a specioid!

A *species* in botanical terms is a group of plants that are naturally occurring and that are capable of breeding together to produce fertile offspring similar to themselves. A species name is in two parts: the first part is the *genus* name (a genus is a group of one or more plants with similar characteristics) and the second the species name, e.g., *Hosta longipes*. A *subspecies* (subsp) is a naturally occurring but distinctly variant population within a species. *Varieties* (var) and *forma* (form) are smaller subdivisions within a species, again occurring naturally. *Cultivars* (cultivated varieties) have been specifically selected or hybridized and can be identified by a name appearing in single quotes, e.g., 'Frances Williams'.

The species *Hosta crispula*, *lancifolia*, *montana*, *nigrescens*, *plantaginea* and *undulata* are featured elsewhere in the text (see chapter 9), but I would like to mention here a few other species. First, because they are very garden worthy, and, second, because it is interesting to have in the garden some of the original species from which many of the cultivars have been bred.

The species *H. fluctuans* was, until recently, generally grown only in Japan. It is now more widely available and is very useful in that it flowers later in the summer than most hostas. It is of a medium size at 24 in. high (60 cm), and has dark, wavy leaves, which are very useful in floral arrangements. It has tall flower scapes (the long flower stalk that comes directly from the roots of the plant) that grow up to 4¼ ft. (130 cm) high, with flowers that are white suffused with violet. It is not commonly grown, not because it lacks appeal, but because it simply has not been widely available. Bred from this species is the wonderful 'Sagae', one of the world's favorite hostas.

H. helonioides is a vigorous hosta that, unlike most, does not mind the sun. It has showy flowers held up high but the plant itself is small at only 15 in. (40 cm), making it very useful for the front of a border. Although the green form is grown, much more popular is the version that has a white edging to the green leaves. This is *H. helonioides* 'Albopicta', which looks a good deal like the cultivar 'Ginko Craig'.

H. hypoleuca is an interesting plant because it has adapted to its natural environment in a most cunning way. In the wild it grows on cliffs and rock faces, which absorb and reflect heat. To protect itself from this heat, the leaves of this species have white undersides. It grows to about 14 in. (35 cm) high, has very large, soft green leaves, and flowers for only a short time. This hosta is considered by many to be one of the loveliest, whether species or cultivar.

H. longipes is fascinating because its name means "long feet." This name is derived from the fact that, in its native habitat, it pushes its roots deep into the cracks of rocks. It is well liked in Japan, but is not readily available elsewhere. I grow a selected form, very possibly a hybrid, called 'Fall Bouquet', which reaches only 8 in. (20 cm) in height and has green pointed leaves.

TOP: H. undulata univittata
ABOVE: H. helonioides 'Albopicta'

H. nakaiana has a Japanese species name that means "ornamental hair-piece" because the flower looks like the traditional hairpin worn by Japanese women. The plant grows to about 12 in. (30 cm) high and is particularly fascinating because all the flower buds are on top of the scape. What is more common in cultivation, and which for a while was thought to be a gold form of *H. nakaiana*, is a hosta I like very much called 'Birchwood Parky's Gold'.

H. sieboldiana is what most people, at least until recently, expect a hosta to be: a plant with big, bold, blue and puckered leaves. It is a superb species, particularly as a background plant, and it favors damp, shady spots. However, what most of us grow is the hybrid *H. sieboldiana* 'Elegans', because its leaves are even more puckered and more blue than the species.

H. tardiflora might well be an impostor, because some authorities think that it could be a cultivar. It has thick, strong green leaves that slugs do not like. Probably its real importance is as a parent of the absolutely beautiful cultivars bred by Eric Smith (1917–1986) of Britain. He crossed *H. sieboldiana* 'Elegans' with *H. tardiflora* to give gardeners a wonderful selection of small blue hostas, the best known being 'Halcyon'.

H. venusta is very small indeed – only about 3 in. (8 cm) high – but it is very pretty. It is used in rock gardens, and is even better when planted in large groups. The flowers, which are a bright mauve, stand tall and make a charming picture.

H. yingeri is interesting in that it was not "discovered" until 1985. It is small, only 6 in. (15 cm) high, and has the most wonderful thick, textured, shiny green leaves that sit flat on the ground. It is very useful for hybridizing, and is an excellent hosta in its own right.

There are of course many more species than those mentioned here and in the rest of this book. Unfortunately, a lot are simply not available or not suitable as garden subjects.

artificial island called Dejima in Nagasaki Harbor, and it became home to the Dutch living in Japan. It was only 130 acres (52 ha) in area, and since no Westerners were permitted to leave, except for an obligatory and difficult journey of 650 miles (1,040 km) once a year to the Shogun in Edo, it seemed like a prison.

Plants were certainly not allowed out of the country. However, a doctor named Englebert Kaempfer (1651–1716), who was intensely interested in botany, made drawings and wrote accounts of hostas around the 1690s. He was probably the first European to see plants from this genus and know what they were.

It was about 80 years after Dr. Kaempfer returned to Amsterdam, that a Swedish doctor named Carl Peter Thunberg (1743–1828) went on behalf of the Dutch East India Company to Japan. He had been a pupil of the famed Carl Linnaeus (inventor of the binomial system of classifying plants and animals), and was vitally interested in studying the plants of other countries. Because of stringent restrictions, only herbarium specimens – that is, dried plant material – could be sent back home. Eventually Thunberg published the classic work *Flora Japonica* (1784), which included descriptions of hostas.

Then came the third of these doctor-botanists, German eye specialist Phillip von Siebold (1796–1867). Eye diseases were endemic in Japan at that time. Von Siebold was a superb teacher and pupils came from all over the country to learn from him at a medical school that trained Japanese students in Western medicine. His reputation was such that he was actually allowed off Dejima and, unbelievably, was eventually permitted to collect botanical specimens. He would not accept payment for his services to the Japanese so his pupils brought him gifts and wrote essays on subjects about which he needed information, including geography, natural history and medicine. He worked 18 hours a day, every day, amassing an enormous botanical collection.

Dr. von Siebold was revered in the Shogun's court and the court authorities gave him a forbidden map of the Japanese coastline. When his term ended, he set sail for Holland with hundreds of crates of plants. On its way back home, the ship was wrecked, the map discovered and von Siebold arrested. The ship eventually sailed again without him and most of the plants perished. Some hostas, however, survived. These were the first actual hosta plants to reach Europe. Two very good and well-known hostas, *Hosta sieboldiana* and *H. sieboldii*, commemorate this extraordinary man.

Von Siebold was pardoned but was banned from returning to Japan for life. On his tombstone, which is Japanese in design, the words "How strong a bridge" are carved in Japanese in tribute to the bridge of knowledge he built between Japan and Europe. He is revered in Japan to this day as a great teacher. We remember him for his introduction of most of the classical hostas.

OPPOSITE: **Hostas showing a variety of shape and color, with** *Disporum variegatum* **in the foreground.**

FOCUS ON FOLIAGE

'Gold Standard'

'Chinese Sunrise'

'Tokudama Aureonebulosa'

'Frances Williams'

'Krossa Regal'

H. fortunei 'Albopicta'

Hostas are beautiful perennial foliage plants with a great diversity of leaf shape, color and size. Hostas have basically eight different leaf shapes, but an individual hosta might incorporate more than one of the following attributes, so the best way to illustrate this diversity is to give examples with accompanying photos.

You can see that some hostas have a mix of leaf shapes. *H. fortunei* 'Albopicta' is cordate, ovate and channeled (the leaves have obvious veins). *H. montana* 'Aureomarginata' is both ovate and oblong. 'Francee' is both ovate and obicular. I will not labor the point, but these examples illustrate how diverse, not to mention beautiful, hosta leaves are.

Hostas come in the basic greens, blues and yellows, as well as a myriad of other variations. More recently, hybridizers have focused on producing more elaborately colored plants that offer a whole new dimension to garden design. Hostas also vary greatly in leaf size: from 'Blue Angel', with leaves of 4 ft. (1.2 m) in length, at one end of the spectrum, to 'Shining Tot' with 2 in. (5 cm) leaves at the other. This gives gardeners tremendous scope in design.

'Summer Haze'

'Carol'

H. montana 'Aureomarginata'

'Francee'

LEAF SHAPE	DESCRIPTION	CULTIVAR ILLUSTRATED
Cordate	heart-shaped	'Gold Standard'
Lanceolate	lance-shaped	'Chinese Sunrise'
Obicular	round	'Tokudama Aureonebulosa'
Obtuse	blunt-pointed	'Decorata'
Oval	curved, with the greatest width in the middle	'Summer Haze'
Ovate	curved, with greatest width above the middle	'Carol'
Rugose	puckered or dimpled	'Frances Williams' (which is also cordate)
Undulate	wavy	'Krossa Regal' (which is also cordate)

TOP: **One of Paul Aden's many popular cultivars, 'Fringe Benefit'.**

Development in North America

After the plant hunters came the hybridizers, those horticulturists who grow and observe different species and cross-breed them in order to develop different shapes, colors and sizes. This is done not necessarily to improve the plant (though they no doubt hope to do so), but to offer greater choice to the gardener.

The first hostas in North America were mentioned as early as 1839 in the *Flower Garden Directory*. Then in the 1870s American Thomas Hogg (1819–92) imported hostas from Japan, while some of von Siebold's plants arrived via England from Holland. By the 1930s the American public had become very interested in hostas and, in response to the new demand, supplies increased. One of the very early hosta authorities in North America was the highly educated Frances Williams, known particularly for the beautiful 'Frances Williams' and for her meticulous work in the observation and cataloging of hostas and disseminating knowledge about the genus.

Countless people and nurseries have contributed to the development of new varieties of hostas over the years. However, a number of American hybridizers and collectors, especially those who have been active in promoting hostas in cultivation, deserve special recognition. Alex J. Summers was co-founder and first president of the American Hosta Society in 1968. He has a large, carefully recorded collection of hostas and has written about them prolifically, including through the *American Hosta Society Bulletin* (later the *Hosta Journal*). Peter Ruh (creator of 'Paul's Glory') was an enthusiast who grew and hybridized many hostas, as were John Grullemns, whose 'Royal Standard' is a stunning classic, Gus Krossa of 'Krossa Regal' fame, Mildred Seaver ('Sea Dream') and Dr. Ralph Benedict ('Salute'). Dr. Warren Pollock has made an enormous contribution as editor of the *American Hosta Journal*, a splendid, interesting and esteemed publication. I have kept my very favorite hybridizer for last. Paul Aden has produced a great number of outstanding varieties, many of them among my best-liked hostas. These include 'Blue Angel', 'Fringe Benefit', 'Wide Brim', 'On Stage', 'Sum and Substance' and many more.

The work of hybridizing has greatly accelerated over the past few years, and now there is a bewildering choice of plants available. Remember, however, that many of the earlier species are just as beautiful as the later, and often brighter, hybrids. A mix of both in the garden is absolutely ideal.

GLOSSARY OF TERMS

albescent	Turning white
crown rot	A fungal disease that occurs in poorly drained soil
cultivar	A specifically bred, cultivated variety
forma	A naturally occurring group within a species
glaucous	A gray-blue waxy appearance to the leaves
hybrid	A plant originating from cross-pollination of two different species
"melt out"	Common term for necrosis in hostas
monocarpic	A plant which flowers only once in its lifetime, then dies
necrosis	Thinning or rotting of some leaves
rugose	Puckered, wrinkled appearance
scape	The stem that bears the flowers
species	A taxonomic classification one level below a genus
sport	A plant showing marked variation from the normal type
variety	A naturally occurring group within a species
viridescent	Turning green

Peter Ruh was an American hosta enthusiast who grew and hybridized many new hosta varieties, including the beautiful 'Paul's Glory'.

TOP: An unnamed seedling.
ABOVE: The pure white flower of *H. plantaginea*.

HOSTA FLOWERS

Some people love hosta flowers, but others can take them or leave them. These plants tend to be grown for their beautiful, diverse leaves and therefore the flowers are not really considered when choosing a hosta. To many gardeners they are a pleasant accessory (although very necessary if we wish to grow hostas from seed).

I think it is fair to say that other than knowing that *H. plantaginea* has beautifully scented flowers, most gardeners would not be able to recognize a hosta by its flower alone, whereas many people can name dozens of actual plants from their leaves. Even the American Hosta Society runs leaf shows where, instead of the whole plant being exhibited, just a single leaf is displayed. They have not, as far as I know, thought of holding a hosta flower show.

Regardless, many hosta flowers are very attractive. The plant blooms for about three weeks (though not every variety at once), after which a great number set seed. The common *H. undulata*, so attractive and easy to grow, has rather sparse flowers that are not very attractive. If you don't want the flowers, you can always chop off the flower scapes. On the other hand, the common little green hosta *H. lancifolia* has a great number of lovely pale lavender flowers that don't necessitate beheading.

Another very common but, I must say, highly regarded hosta is *H. ventricosa*, which has green leaves and really attractive purple flowers. These are particularly worthwhile because the whole spike opens at once, so you do not get that annoying habit of the bottom flowers dying off before the top ones open. Variants of the same species have the same type of flower, for example, *H. ventricosa* 'Aureomarginata' and *H. ventricosa* 'Aureomaculata'.

Those in the *H. sieboldiana* group are certainly some of the most spectacular hostas as far as leaves are concerned, but their white flowers are not very tall and tend to look insignificant. On the other hand, the stunning *H. nigrescens* looks out of proportion when it

A variety of hosta flower shapes and colors. *CLOImage removed.CKWISE FROM ABOVE LEFT: H. sieboldiana* 'Elegans', *H. ventricosa*, 'Lady Isobel Barnett', 'Lakeside Accolade'.

flaunts its tall flower scapes; however, others might think it is splendidly architectural. The Tokudama group are like smaller sieboldianas: they have lots of flowers all bunched up at the top of the scape, which is actually much prettier than it sounds.

The *H. montana* group have tall scapes of lavender flowers, whereas the *H. sieboldii* group contain big differences in both color and size.

Flowers of the *H. plantaginea* are easy to recognize because the scented blossoms are white, and the beautiful (but a little difficult to grow) 'Aphrodite' has double flowers that truly are stunning.

Some hostas have beautiful bracts (a modified leaf from whose base a flower grows) at the top of the flower scape, and I am inclined to think that these are more attractive than the eventual flower. Most hosta flowers are pretty when they first come out, and not so pretty later – but that could be true of many flowers. What I do is cut them down when they are past their best. Of course if you wish to grow from seed you will need to leave them alone. This can look both natural and attractive when stems are bearing fattening seed pods.

Since hostas come with flowers we might as well appreciate them, but I do not really choose hostas for anything but their leaves.

Cultivation

Planting

Before you plant any garden subject you need to choose a suitable place where it will be happy to grow. For hostas, dappled shade in a woodland-type setting is ideal. It has been suggested that you can grow them in lots of sun if the soil is kept moist, but this is not a theory to which I subscribe. Yes, they will grow, but not well. They will undoubtedly get scorched and, in many cases, particularly those with a lot of pale coloring to their leaves, they will simply frizzle up. If you are going to grow something, grow it in suitable conditions. If your site is hot and sunny, grow gerberas! It is just a matter of being realistic. Do not despair if you cannot provide suitable shade. Containers can usually be placed in a shady spot, and a collection of hostas in containers can look wonderful (see chapter 7).

When to plant

The seasons for planting hostas are spring and fall. I favor spring, when the plant has the very best chance of settling in and making optimum growth before winter. Also, the spring season is when you may select from the potted plants in garden centers, before they get that tired look caused by unsuitable conditions and, quite often, erratic care. If you are taking divisions from the plants you already have, spring is the time to do this as well. (We will discuss how to do this in the next chapter; see page 34.)

OPPOSITE: A woodland setting with dappled shade and a moist environment is ideal for hostas.

RIGHT: A shady bank is a great location for hostas and their companion plants.

Having promoted spring, it must be said that the planting can be accomplished in the fall also, but in these cooler conditions you could be faced with root rot, and small divisions are likely to perish. While it is possible to plant in summer, the amount of water a newly planted hosta requires makes it quite hard work to keep the soil suitably moist during this season.

How to plant

Planting instructions for hostas are much the same as for any other plant. Once you have chosen your site, make a hole bigger than the plant itself, fill the bottom of the hole with well-rotted manure or compost, then add some loamy soil on top. Place your plant in the hole. Fill around the plant with soil, gently firming it in place with a hand or foot. Water well.

After planting, observe with pleasure the rapid growth of your hosta, especially if you have planted it early in the spring so as to catch the first surge of growth. If your climate is dry, you will need to make sure that the plants are kept moist through their first summer season.

Transplanting

Your hosta will not show its full potential for a year or two. As it matures its leaves will get bigger and the clump size will increase. If you find later that the hosta has outgrown its allotted space you can simply move it, either in spring or early fall, before any frost occurs. At these times, you might also consider dividing the plant to make more (see page 34).

The best results are obtained by leaving your plant undisturbed to grow in beauty with the years. Sometimes this is not possible, because it is often difficult to judge the eventual size of a hosta. Books and catalogs will give you some idea of plant size, but climate and cultivation differences can cause plant size to vary, so use this information as a guide only.

Shade requirements

The good news about hostas is that they are very easy to grow, provided they have conditions that suit them. In a nutshell, hostas need shade and moisture, so do not try to grow them on a sunny, dry hillside alongside your daisies. Most gardens have some shade provided by trees and shrubs, and this dappled light is absolutely ideal for hostas. Beautiful plantings can be created by combining hostas with complementary shade-loving subjects. A shady border of mixed trees and shrubs or a bed on the shady side of the house is all you need for your hostas.

Do not despair if you don't have such a shady area, because there are other ways you can grow hostas. One such way is in containers (see chapter 7), which can be moved to take advantage of shade. A second way is to provide artificial shade. This can be created by using a shadehouse – made with materials that will

TOP: Newly planted hosta seedlings with plenty of space left for the adult plants to develop.

ABOVE LEFT: *H. crispula* recently transplanted into a well-mulched bed.

ABOVE RIGHT: The results of sun damage on a hosta's leaves.

blend unobtrusively into the landscape – or by using shade cloth, although it can sometimes look unsightly when it is not incorporated into a proper structure. Another approach is to select cultivars that are more tolerant of the sun.

Soil and mulch

Hostas prefer a moist, friable loam that is slightly acidic (a pH of 6 is ideal). To this you should add plenty of organic matter. I favor well-rotted manure – in my case, I use sheep manure – in which the hostas really thrive. Hostas are plants that have to be fed to look their best, so compost is important, in addition to some slow-release fertilizer and a little blood meal and bone meal. This is best applied in the spring, ideally just before growth commences.

Mulch is wonderful for keeping the moisture in the soil where it is needed. I particularly like hay, straw or mushroom compost, but leaf mold is also very good. If you apply mulch in late fall to early winter, having first tidied up the beds, you will find that any weeds that grow in spring can very easily be removed. Should you live in a cool climate, it is wise to keep the mulch back from the hostas' crowns in case they rot. In really cold climates, where snow or very heavy frost is common, make the mulch a good deal deeper.

When you provide all these nutrients and moisture to your hostas, they will reward you by growing profusely. They will also help to prevent weeds from appearing. While hostas need to be fed as described, there is no need to make a big fuss over them. Hostas are perennials that truly are "easy care."

Pests

I don't enjoy either reading or writing about pests and diseases but you have to know what you are up against! Slugs and snails are the worst and most persistent pests for hostas. Some gardeners suggest using poisons, others prefer the organic approach of scattering eggshells, ashes or bark. Unfortunately the latter solutions are not always effective, but often gardeners are willing to put up with chewed leaves to avoid using pesticides. Whatever approach you take, you need to devise a program for the whole season, not just in the spring. Perhaps most importantly, maintaining good garden hygiene will help to ensure that there are fewer breeding places for slugs and snails, whose eggs are usually found under sheltering leaves, even under hostas rotting down at the end of the season. So always tidy up the garden bed before adding mulch. Like it or not, pellets or sprays are the best solution for getting rid of slugs and snails. However, as mentioned above, if you are willing to put up with leaf damage you may be able to find a balance using organic methods. When using poisons there is always the anxiety that these may kill birds or pets, but there are pelletized poisons available that guarantee not to hurt anything but your target pest. The most common poisons contain metaldehyde in various amounts as the active ingredient , but new products are coming on

OPPOSITE: 'Blue Mammoth' responding in spectacular fashion to a suitable site.

BELOW: The damage caused by slugs and snails snacking on a hosta.

THREE DIFFICULT BEAUTIES

Lest you think hostas are just too easy to grow (and most of them are), I want to tell you about 'Frances Williams', 'Aurora Borealis' and 'Samurai'. These breathtakingly beautiful hostas have deeply corrugated, glaucous leaves, heavily margined in yellow. They are very similar, and in the early spring you will be amazed at how lovely they are. The problem with these three cultivars is that they can suffer from necrosis. To try to prevent this from developing, I plant them in a very shady place. This seems to help, but even if I have trouble later, the early season display is so gorgeous that I am willing to take a chance on necrosis.

If you really want to try your luck in growing 'Frances Williams' I suggest planting a stunning display of candelabra primula among them, in as many colors as you can find (see the description in chapter 8). I particularly recommend *Primula pulverulenta* (zones 4–8) in crimson-red and *P. japonica* 'Miller's Crimson' (zones 3–8). If your hostas are less than perfect, this will give a glorious display of color that will divert your attention.

TOP: 'Aurora Borealis'
ABOVE: 'Frances Williams'
RIGHT: 'Samurai'

to the market all the time. Iron phosphate is used in some slug and snail poisons and is less toxic, though also less effective, than metaldehyde-based products. Another possibility is to try coffee grounds or a caffeine solution around the plants you want to protect. Caffeine has been shown to be effective at both killing and deterring slugs and snails and, while toxic to some beneficial insects, it is safer for pets and humans using the garden.

It is absolutely critical to use whatever method you have chosen to protect your hostas before the new shoots emerge in spring, otherwise the leaves will be disfigured before you even notice what is happening. From then on, keep up the program of protection. Even if you use long-life poison pellets, you must keep using them on a regular basis. Hostas that appear pristine in the spring often become sadly chewed by the summer when a gardener has forgotten the pest-culling program. Slugs and snails are unrelenting.

There are other pests in the garden also, including perhaps rabbits, deer and voles, depending on where you live. If you have a garden, you are probably already dealing with these larger pests through trapping or poisoning, if local regulations permit, or by fencing them out. Often, it is a case of living with these larger animals and protecting your garden as best you can.

Diseases

Hostas are generally healthy plants and do not suffer much from disease. One problem worth mentioning is crown rot, which can occur if you have poorly drained soil. If you see yellow leaves where no such color should be, be alert to this possible cause. When you pull these leaves, they come away easily and have a nasty smell. When this happens, dig up the plant immediately, cut away the rotten bits, and soak the remaining healthy part in a bucket of fungicide for a few hours. After that you should put it in a pot and keep it away from other plants until next season. If the plant appears diseased when all those around it are flourishing, don't waste time on it – throw it out!

The first signs of necrosis, a problem that seems to occur early in the growing season.

The other problem that can be of concern is necrosis, commonly called "melt-out." This is not actually a disease but the disintegration of large areas of pale-colored leaves. This problem seems to happen only early in the season and may be caused by the weather. From observation and experience, I find that rapid changes in temperature and humidity, as well as damp weather, can influence melt-out. This disfigurement occurs in only a few hostas including such beauties as 'Frances Williams', with its cream margins, and 'Samurai'. Since it is a problem only early in the season, if you remove the affected leaves quickly, the replacements have a better chance of surviving. The American Hosta Society's darling 'Frances Williams', top of the popularity polls for many years, has fallen from grace because of this problem. Currently, there is no known solution for melt-out.

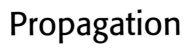

Propagation

Raising from seed

There are literally hundreds of hosta cultivars and varieties to choose from, so why would you bother to grow them from seed? There are probably various reasons: perhaps it is just for the fun of seeing if you can do it; maybe you have an extensive area you wish to plant with hostas, but you don't have an extensive budget to match; or perhaps, at the back of your mind, you think you just might produce something unique.

Dealing with the last reason first, the great British hosta expert Diana Grenfell says that most seedling hostas are not worth growing. This seems to be a rather harsh statement, but I think she means that unless you make deliberate crosses through hand-pollination (and for this you need to be armed with a certain amount of botanical know-how) you will, in her opinion, not grow anything worthwhile. If the would-be hybridizer is trying to replicate the plant form from which the seed was gathered, as she rightly points out, even species will not come true to type because hostas interbreed so readily. However, this is not what most of us are aiming for when we grow hostas from seed. We just want to see what happens when we plant seed from open-pollinated plants.

I understand that the well-known American hybridizer Mildred Seaver let her plants seed freely in the garden and then fight for survival. The fittest were then evaluated and some splendid new cultivars were named. W. George

OPPOSITE: Propagating hostas from seed or dividing them is a great way to increase numbers when you want to plant up a big area.

RIGHT: In the foreground is the author's own selected seedling 'Biddy's Blue'.

A green seedling that appeared in the author's garden.

POLLINATION

Hybridized plants, i.e., plants that have been bred and selected for certain characteristics, do not come true to type (i.e., don't retain the characteristics of the parent plant) from seed. The same is true of unusual growth forms, such as sports and mutations. In the case of hostas, because the species interbreed so readily and if you have two or more species in your garden they will cross-pollinate, even species do not necessarily produce identical offspring. So, if you want an identical plant, you need to propagate by division.

If, however, variation is not important to you or you want to try your hand at producing a new hybrid, growing hostas from seed can be a lot of fun. There are two approaches to hybridizing from seed: using seed from open pollination and using seed from hand pollination. The first allows plants to cross-pollinate freely with other hostas in the garden, meaning a great variety is produced in the offspring. The second involves selecting the parent plants and taking the ripe pollen of one and placing it on the stigma of the other. This is an involved process and beyond the scope of this book, but specialized books on propagation would be a good place to start if you want to pursue this technique further.

Schmid, author of the classic book *The Genus Hosta*, has this to say on the subject of propagating hostas from seed: "While raising hostas from random pollinated seed is fascinating and a worthwhile activity, it must be stated that most of the seedlings will not be outstanding hostas and are not worth naming, although they may be useful in mass planting or ground cover."

My husband has mostly blue, green or gold (a few) hostas, some blotched and none variegated. Only one turned out to be worth naming, the heavily textured, glaucous 'Summer Haze'. Another seedling he raised that shows promise is called 'Ace of Hearts'; it is blue and puckered, with heart-shaped leaves and pleasing pale lavender flowers. For the others, he has done as Dr. Schmid suggested and made a splendid mass planting. Although none of the other hostas raised merited naming, they have still been useful in allowing a large area to be planted. It would have cost a great deal of money to have done this with named varieties. Over time the least attractive plants can be judiciously removed and superior, named varieties put in their place.

Hybridizing any plant depends on the botanical knowledge of the person making the crosses. It is really like breeding horses or cattle – it is necessary to understand the performance of a breeding line and how it is liable to interact with another. This should not deter you from trying to cross-breed if you really want to and, who knows, you might strike gold.

Seed sowing

It is very easy to grow hostas from seed. Gather the seed just as the capsules begin to turn yellow and put them somewhere sunny to dry. After a while, the capsules will split and the seeds can be cleaned. The black seeds are fertile; the rest can be discarded. The seeds can be used right away, and although it is not necessary to break dormancy, stratification (a period of cool temperatures to

Unnamed seedlings, the result of allowing hostas to hybridize and seed freely.

break dormancy) in a refrigerator for up to six weeks can help improve the rate of successful germination.

The seeds need to be sown in temperatures of around 65°F (18°C). If necessary, you can sow the seeds in pots in a greenhouse, but make sure you spray them with a fungicide to make sure they don't suffer from "damping off" (a fungal problem common to seedlings grown in a moist atmosphere). You might also consider waiting until spring and planting them in open ground under shade frames. You can also plant seeds in the fall, but they will not germinate until spring when the ground warms up. When they appear will depend on your climate.

Sow the seeds thinly because with hostas every seed seems to have a strong ambition to grow, so you can get a tremendous number of plants appearing. If the seedlings are greenhouse-grown, use a good commercial seed-raising mix and feed during the growing season with an all-purpose 10-10-10 liquid fertilizer. Seedlings will be ready to be transplanted into individual containers when the little plants have four leaves. Those seedlings grown under shade frames or directly in the garden will have to be thinned out regularly and replanted to give them space to grow.

You will need to continue to re-pot as necessary for some time because it is difficult to judge a hosta's worth until it reaches maturity, at about one year of age. Of course, then you have the problem of what to do with the "rejects."

Vegetative propagation

When you want some more hostas you can divide those you already have, which is a sensible and cheap way of increasing your stock. If you own only the very common hostas you can, of course, split them, but do not forget that it's a good idea to buy new cultivars so that your collection grows in beauty and variety. These new plants can, in turn, be divided as well. I would suggest that you buy two or three new hostas each year, which, once mature, can be split and divided annually.

Dividing your plant

If you have a big clump of hostas in your garden, in the early spring, when the shoots are just showing, arm yourself with a freshly sharpened spade and cut a wedge out of the plant, making sure there are a number of healthy roots attached. You may well crush a spear or two, but with care very little damage is caused. Lift out the slice, and replace the soil in the hole you have created. Then you can either plant the one piece you have chopped off, or you can divide it further to get more plants. If you are going to do the latter, hose all the soil off so you can see where you can best cut – you want the most plants for the least damage. Discard your spade and use a sharp knife

The new shoots of *H. undulata*.

for this operation. Once planted, keep the hostas watered for a few days and they will reward you by growing away merrily. This is the simplest method of propagation and, of course, you know exactly what you are getting, unlike when you grow hostas from seed.

The "roundabout" method of propagation

There is another method of adding to your hosta collection that I have not seen mentioned in books. It is called swapping or exchanging your plants, and may be done on a one-to-one basis or as a group activity. You do not necessarily have to exchange oranges for oranges, so to speak. You might want someone's 'Whirlwind', while the owner of this flamboyant hosta might covet your *Trillium lutea*. It would always be a fair swap if both parties were satisfied.

You might consider starting a local group whose common interest is growing hostas. The group could meet in the different members' gardens in order to examine what treasures they have. Then you can decide what treasure of your own would secure that unusual, desirable plant you have seen. It sounds like fun, and even if you have only two or three hosta-growing friends, you could still exchange pieces of your plants and all have better gardens for the effort.

Micropropagation is used to produce thousands of perfect copies of the parent plant, in this case the lovely 'June'.

Landscaping with Hostas: Color Selections for Borders and Beds

For mixed borders

Most people plant hostas in mixed borders and beds, utilizing the shady areas and growing them in association with other plants. This can be a very attractive approach, and is within the reach of a great many gardeners. However, it is always said that, whatever the variety, plants are better placed in groups. From experience, I believe this is certainly true, although if your garden is small this is not always practical, unless you are satisfied growing a very restricted number of cultivars.

If your border is a good size you have various options with regard to hostas, including a very wide range of shapes, sizes and colors to choose from. If you like a little formality, you might like to edge your border with a small-growing variety, which could be either plain or fancy. In blue you could use 'Blue Moon' or 'Hadspen Blue', 'Blue Cadet' or 'Halcyon'. In gold, you might like 'Gold Edger', 'Golden Prayers' or 'Golden Medallion'.

For a really strong visual effect in a border edging, try variegated hostas. It would be difficult to fault 'Golden Tiara' in this category; its green leaves edged with gold are very pretty indeed. 'Chinese Sunrise' has leaves with chartreuse centers and narrow dark green edges and would also be suitable. When it comes

OPPOSITE: Hostas make a dramatic addition to a large mixed planting garden bed. *ABOVE LEFT:* 'Golden Tiara' used as a border edging. *ABOVE RIGHT:* The wonderful blue of small-growing 'Hadspen Blue', which makes an ideal edger.

THIS PAGE: The contrast of the seasons. At left are the vigorous new shoots of spring, and the hostas slowly dying back before the onset of winter.

OPPOSITE: Four hostas in the full flush of summer, flanked by fall scenes as hosta leaves c color and die back.

SEASONAL CHANGES

The older I get the more I realize how rewarding it is to watch plants closely and to appreciate all facets of growth – not just the obvious beauty of the plant in full flush. This is perhaps because now I seem to have more time, or possibly more inclination to study growing plants at all stages instead of impatiently waiting until they are fully grown.

Well, you might say, that is all very well, but how do you appreciate a hosta garden (by which I mean one devoted solely to hostas) in the winter? The answer lies in both the outward and inward eye. The outward eye sees the neat bed, smothered with fallen leaves, mulch or possibly snow and ice, the deciduous trees that provide shelter in summer standing stark, their branches making intricate patterns. The inward eye sees the beauty that will come, and anticipation is a very pleasurable activity. So sit by the fire, read plant catalogs and plan your spring extravagances.

Early in the spring the first shoots of hostas appear. Look at them closely because they are beautiful in themselves and so vulnerable that you cannot imagine how they are to grow into such robust and gorgeous plants. Not all shoots are the same: some are fat and purple, some are skinny and green, some look like fat spears of asparagus. You cannot guess by looking at these early shoots what they will be – green, gold or variegated. Then gradually the excitement builds as leaves start to unfurl. This is a particularly attractive stage, just before the full glory of the plant is displayed.

Now is the time to examine the intricacy of individual leaves. In North America the American Hosta Society holds leaf shows, where instead of the whole plant you just enter your best leaf into the competition. This seems very sensible since, with hostas, the leaves are the thing. You would not expect to dig up your whole rose bush to display a bloom, or expect an entire camellia plant to win "best in show" for its bloom. The other good thing about leaf shows is that they concentrate your attention on the actual beauty of just one leaf, separate from the plant and from any beauty-enhancing background or companion plants. While you might look at the most colorful leaf first, eventually you will find it rewarding to look at all the others. Hosta leaves display a quiet beauty even though their colors may be intense deep blue or various shades of green, lemon, yellow or gold. Their rugose, puckered or veined leaves may well show more clearly when your eye is not distracted by multiple colors.

Spring and summer are of course the seasons of glory, but what about fall? In the autumn, the leaves of the departing hostas turn yellow, and if you haven't already removed the flower scapes they will stand stark and dry. For the most part, fall just seems to be a timely reminder that the major housekeeping tasks of the year are about to begin.

to green and white small-growing hostas, you might like the tried-and-true *H. crispula*, 'Decorata' or 'Ginko Craig'. If your border is bright with perennial or annual color, quieter-colored hostas create areas of tranquility and can be used to divide one color from another. Blue and green varieties do this well.

Although hosta leaves come in a wide range of colors to suit almost any planting scheme, it must be mentioned here that hosta colors do not remain the same throughout a whole season. A blue may change to green, yellow to chartreuse, and bright yellows may sometimes turn white. Certainly the loveliest colors appear in the spring, but this does not mean that later changes are unacceptable – it's just that they are usually not as striking.

Blue selection

Blue hostas are universally popular, and recurring groups of three or five plants through a border can tie the various components together and make a cohesive whole. The restful blues also provide a break between the brighter colors of other subjects.

If your mixed border is large, my first choice would be *H. sieboldiana* 'Elegans' because its splendid foliage is puckered, resembling seersucker, and stoutly rounded and is consequently of enormous merit in the garden. These plants grow to about 36 in. (60 cm) high and just over 48 in. (120 cm) wide. In my opinion the flowers of 'Elegans' have an advantage

Two blue hostas suitable for a blue border. Right is *H. sieboldiana* 'Elegans', which is suitable for a large border. If you want something smaller-growing, try 'Tokudama' (opposite).

over other cultivars in that they are white and barely appear above the leaves. Often hosta scapes grow too tall and look out of proportion to the plant.

If you think that 'Elegans' would grow too large for your garden, there is a smaller-growing blue that is one of the most beautiful of hostas – 'Tokudama'. It is like a small version of 'Elegans', and one of the bluest of the hostas. It is also slower growing than 'Elegans' and has thick, deeply cupped and heavily textured leaves. These two hostas are said to be resistant to slug and snail damage, but I wouldn't rely on this.

Other blue hostas that are both beautiful and work well in a border, as their size does not overwhelm other plants, are 'Birchwood Blue', 'Abiqua Drinking Gourd', 'Love Pat', 'Buckshaw Blue', 'Blue Wedgwood' and 'Blue Seer'. There are other blues that would suit, depending on your taste and their availability. (For more suggestions see chapter 5.)

The varieties mentioned above are in general cultivation, but if you contact a specialist mail-order nursery you might find some rare or unusual plants to suit your taste. If you plan to buy more than one of a variety, I advise you to be prudent and purchase a variety that is tried and true so that you will not be disappointed in its performance. If it is something new that sounds great, is very expensive and rare, don't buy more than one until its performance in your garden can be assessed. Experts say this can take five years, but I think a couple of years would be enough for most gardeners.

Green selection

You will find a great number of green hostas, so the choice can be bewildering, especially since there are so many different greens; some are dark, some are light, while the leaf shape can be round, pointed, heart-shaped, plain, puckered or lined. Size, as with any hosta, can be large, medium or small. So how do you choose? If possible it is a good idea to actually see a collection of hostas, perhaps in your local garden center or in a garden that specializes in them. If you cannot manage this, you will have to rely on books or growers' catalogs. Certainly, the more you see of this stunning perennial the more you realize just how diverse in color, shape and size the genus is (and the closer you are to becoming an avid collector).

Green is particularly restful, so hostas in this color can tone down brighter colors (if that is what you want) or blend beautifully with other foliage. I will first mention a hosta that I hold in the highest regard. Called 'Krossa Regal', it is tall, graceful and rather like a vase in shape. I am not the only one who thinks this hosta is special; in 1988 it placed second in the American Hosta Society's popularity poll. Not only is its shape pleasing, but the leaves have a very thick texture and are deeply veined. Different again, but very worthwhile, is 'Invincible', which has bright, shiny green leaves of a very thick texture. As a bonus, its white flowers are fragrant.

Sometimes I think we are inclined to forget the species hostas in favor of more modern hybrids. Other plants, for example, rhododendrons, suffer the same fate. There is often a mistaken idea that hybrids are superior to their ancestors. This is not true, of course, for sometimes the simplicity of the species can offer something that is lacking in the often more brightly colored hybrids. Therefore I recommend planting the splendid species *H. montana*. In the wild it has a very wide distribution in its native Japan and is quite variable, which botanists find a challenge. It would be difficult not to appreciate this extremely large (36 in./90 cm high), majestic hosta with its green, deeply veined leaves. It would need to be placed at the back of the border because of its size.

I understand that what we know as *H. fortunei* is a botanist's nightmare, as there is doubt about it being a species. However, whether species or not, the plant that goes by this name is a nice green hosta, 14–18 in. (35–45 cm) high with rather rounded leaves and pretty lavender flowers.

Next comes the species *H. ventricosa*, which British expert Diana Grenfell calls "one of the best flowering plants in the genus and one of the best green-leafed hostas, being of good poise and shape." Make sure you don't overlook this one.

A hosta called 'Green Fountain' is aptly named and its cascading leaves make a very good contrast in form. If you want a very tall background plant, 'Jade Cascade' is ideal. If its growing conditions are right, it can reach up to 36 in. (90 cm) in height.

The green hostas suggested are all readily available.

OPPOSITE: H. fortunei makes a nice addition to the green border.
BELOW: 'Invincible' has bright, shiny green leaves that will add a fresh splash of color to any border.

ABOVE: The gold tones of 'Zounds' can be appreciated in this close-up of the leaves.

RIGHT: Surrounded by green and blue hostas, 'Piedmont Gold' demonstrates how a gold hosta can add a spark to the garden.

Gold selection

Gold is such a pretty color, somehow satisfactory in its richness, and is very versatile in the garden. It can contrast with blues and greens, and works well on its own as a group planting with real impact. When speaking of gold hostas, yellow, which is equally useful though not so intense in color, should also be included here.

Gold and yellow hostas need more shade than blues and greens. As I have mentioned, most hostas need shade, especially from the afternoon sun. Early morning sun, however, is just fine. Complete shade does not suit many plants, and although hostas probably will not die in such circumstances, they certainly will not thrive. Therefore, if you plan to have gold and yellow hostas in your mixed border, place them in shaded areas.

Having said this, there is one outstanding exception. Called 'Sum and Substance', this is one of my favorite hostas. It is very large – 30 in. (75 cm) high and 60 in. (150 cm) wide – and is a very beautiful chartreuse color. If it is exposed to some sun (i.e., at least half the time) it turns yellow. Its large heavy leaves make a truly splendid display. If planting it in your mixed border, allow plenty of space to show its full potential. A group of five or so is an awesome sight. Aside from its beauty, it has another virtue – slugs and snails do not care for it. In any scale of worth it would be ten out of ten, and in the hosta world I think it is the height of perfection.

From the same well-known breeder (Paul Aden of Baldwin, New York) comes a very beautiful cultivar called 'Zounds'. A brilliant gold with handsome puckered leaves, this hosta's brightness really glows, and it is most useful in the shadiest parts of a border.

A newer gold hosta that is very striking with its large pointed leaves is called 'Glory'. Once again, a group of these plants looks very impressive, but if you plan on only using one among your blues and greens it still plays an important role.

'Sun Power' is a very pretty gold with a graceful growth habit. The only problem is that, despite its name, it does not like much sun and needs to be grown in a fairly shady spot, with just early morning sun.

A very good, quite large hosta is 'August Moon'. It starts off as a pale green, then turns a soft pale gold. Even toward the end of the season it remains very fresh-looking.

With their changing colors throughout the season, hostas are always interesting and a hosta display is never static. Gold hostas usually stay substantially the same in color, unless they are exposed to too much sun, in which case they may scorch. A very desirable gold that likes a good deal of shade is 'Piedmont Gold'. Its aversion to the sun is advantageous to gardeners because it can survive in areas that are too shady for most plants. It could be planted alongside 'Sun Power', as they enjoy the same conditions.

The gold hostas mentioned so far are not small, but there are some little hostas in yellow and gold that are well worth growing and can take their place at the front of a mixed border. My favorite is a little charmer called 'Blond Elf'. It is soft yellow and only about 8 in. (20 cm) high. It makes a nice rounded mound of 24 in. (60 cm) and is very neat, tidy and compact. 'Golden Prayers' is a little taller, and if you use your imagination the upright-growing leaves may remind you of praying hands. The name 'Gold Edger' says it all, and this hosta possesses the great virtue of spreading rapidly, while 'Golden Scepter' is a yellow form of the ever-popular 'Golden Tiara'. 'Little Aurora' is one of the smallest of the gold-leafed varieties, and it increases rapidly.

There are, of course, more gold and yellow hostas than those I have mentioned, but these are the varieties that I like best, not only for their beauty, but also because of their strong performance in the garden. They are all readily available from good hosta sources.

Variegated selection

In the past 20 years there has been an astonishing upsurge of interest in hostas. This has meant that hybridizers have been encouraged to breed more and more varieties. Since the first species introduced were mostly blue and green (although a few had white margins), they have worked to produce brighter colors, be they variegated or margined. While the hosta's colors – blue, green, gold and yellow – have not changed, what is different is the way they have been arranged on the leaves. Some of the results have

TOP: **The stunning gold, green and blue tones of 'Great Expectations'.**
ABOVE: 'Francee'

ABOVE: *H. fortunei* 'Albopicta' is a medium grower with a striking creamy leaf.

LEFT: 'Gene's Joy'

been nothing short of spectacular, making selection either a real problem or real fun, depending on how you look at it.

There are three sorts of "multicolored" hostas. One is the variegated-margin group, which have dark leaf color with white or yellow margins. The second is the variegated-center group, which is the reverse of the first, having a paler color in the leaf center, with darker edges. These to me are some of the most exciting and beautiful of all hostas, and I describe more of my favorite medio-variegated hostas, as they are sometimes called, on pages 62 and 72. The third group have irregularly variegated leaves with striped or blotched streaks, usually on a darker-colored background. Some of these tend to be unstable and will revert to a solid color. Many of these kinds I find to be more novel than beautiful.

Later in this chapter we'll discuss the idea of a hosta walk, which gives great scope for using all shapes, forms and colors of hosta, but for the mixed border or bed it is important to be selective in choosing plants, so that what is planted will blend rather than dominate.

Green or blue hostas with white or cream margins have an important place in the mixed border. It would be difficult to neglect 'Francee' because it looks so crisp and fresh, but there are many others, some rather more dramatic. 'Abba Dabba Do', with its dark green leaves edged in gold, is larger, so would need to take up residence in the back of the bed. 'Iona' is smaller but striking, with strong, creamy margins that do not change color during the season. 'Treasure Trove' and 'Sunny Smiles' would also fit in well.

For something dramatic you cannot ignore there is 'Pizzazz', which is frosted blue-green with waxy, creamy white margins. 'Antioch' is showy in green and white and is a plant that has been highly regarded for many years. Another hosta that is not quite so showy but still very desirable is 'Frosted Jade'. All three of these grow quite large – up to 32 in. (80 cm) in height.

'Moonlight' is a medium grower with a white edge around the leaves, as is 'Shade Fanfare', and the very pretty H. fortunei 'Albopicta' has a cream leaf with a green margin. These colors fade to a blend of greens later in the season, but I would still recommend them.

When it comes to choosing from the medio-variegated group for a mixed border there are many hostas now available, and it is to be hoped that you can view some of them in your garden center. 'Color Glory' has a yellow center with wide, irregular blue margins. It is large and very beautiful, though I have found it to be quite a slow grower. 'Midwest Magic' is new and desirable, with a yellow center edged in green, and 'Gene's Joy' is very prettily marked with the green margin streaking into the creamy chartreuse center. Among the small growers, 'Emerald Tiara' fits with a gold color scheme and is a very reliable plant.

TOP: 'So Sweet'

ABOVE: 'Tokudama Flavocircinalis'

There are so many more variegated hostas that are suitable for a mixed border, and some of my favorites include the following. 'Tokudama Aureonebulosa' is a gem that has a cloudy yellow center with an irregular margin of gorgeous glaucous blue. It is very subtly colored and remains lovely all season. 'Lucy Vitols' is another splendid choice. It has a yellowish green center with an irregular green margin and attractive puckered leaves that turn more golden as the season advances. My third choice, to make a very select trio, is 'Fragrant Bouquet', which also has a wide yellow center with a green edge.

In hostas I love the color known as chartreuse, which is neither green nor yellow but somewhere in between. A very fine example of this is 'Guacamole', which has apple-green margins and a chartreuse center. Its coloring is very restful, as is that of *H. fortunei* 'Albopicta', whose green margin is quite bright in the beginning, but gradually turns green and chartreuse, which is prettier, I think, than the original coloring. A small grower in chartreuse with a narrow green margin is 'Chinese Sunrise' and this variety also fades to a quieter color in the summer. Although 'September Sun' does not turn chartreuse, it would fit into this group very well. Its leaves have a wide yellow center and a green margin, but the colors are soft.

There are a great number of hostas that have green centers and yellow margins, some of which are very striking. The really bright ones are probably best left out of the mixed border, but I would certainly include some that would enhance other plants rather than overwhelm them. In this category I would include 'So Sweet', 'Tokudama Flavocircinalis', 'Fringe Benefit', 'Golden Scepter' and 'Wide Brim'. These are all good-quality, medium-sized, yellow-margined hostas that are a real pleasure to grow.

For a white garden

Some years ago it was the fashion for gardeners to have a white garden; obviously this could not be exclusively white, but it was basically white and green. The idea was rather done to death for a while, but in fact such gardens can be stunning if carefully designed. Hostas have a place in white gardens, especially if they are a plain green, or are green with white or cream edges.

Some dramatic green-and-white hostas for a white garden

To enhance your white garden, you should consider green hostas with some white or pale cream in the leaves (cream usually turns white as the season advances). These would look very good planted either as single specimens or in groups.

There are more hostas with blue-lavender flowers than with white, so if you are a real purist you would need to restrict yourself to those with white

OPPOSITE: A large white woodland garden.

Three wonderful green-and-white hostas for a white garden. From top: 'Minuteman', 'Spearmint', 'Sunny Smiles'.

blooms – or you might like to cut off the flowers. Alternatively, you could heed the words of the famous English gardener Gertrude Jekyll (1843–1932): "It is a curious thing that people will sometimes spoil some garden project for the sake of a word. For instance, a blue garden for beauty's sake may be hankering for a group of white lilies, or something in the palest lemon yellow, but is not allowed to have it because it is called the blue garden, and there must be no other flowers." Translate "blue garden" into "white garden," and you might want to consider leaving the blue-lavender hosta flowers to add some contrast to your white theme.

The following green-and-white hostas are very dramatic, and would certainly make a statement. 'Patriot' is green with a very wide white margin, making it look fresh and spontaneous. It is a vigorous grower, as is its cousin 'Minuteman'. In fact, they are so alike they are almost indistinguishable. Another close relative called 'Fire and Ice' has a reverse coloration so that the white is in the center and the green is on the outside. Two others that share similar coloration are 'Night Before Christmas' and 'White Christmas'. These would all be wonderful in groups if your garden is large enough. Otherwise, just one of each would add tremendous interest to a white garden.

Other selections for a white garden

Next are some hostas that are not quite so dramatic but which are still beautiful additions to a white garden. There is a wide choice available but I would recommend sticking to the following plants, whose green leaves are margined white. One of the most familiar is the tried-and-true 'Decorata', also known as *H. decorata* or 'Thomas Hogg'. But "a rose by any other name would smell as sweet," so under whichever name you purchase this hosta, you will find it is crisp and reliable, appearing early in the spring. 'Francee' is a deservedly popular hosta, as are 'Iona', 'Emily Dickinson' and 'Northern Halo'. All are green with white edges and have a very neat and tidy habit. (There is even a hosta called 'Neat and Tidy', but it does not have a white margin!) There is also 'Brim Cup', which has very puckered leaves, 'Carol', with nicely rounded leaves, 'Twilight', which always looks fresh, and the lovely 'Sunny Smiles'. Should you want to plant a small-growing front-of-the-border type, try 'Allan P. McConnell' or the pretty little 'Diamond Tiara'.

Naturally, you do not have to slavishly follow my suggestion of having only green-and-white hostas in your white garden. I think that the soft green of *H. plantaginea* and its form 'Aphrodite', although they don't have white margins on their leaves, are beautiful, and they have white flowers that are attractively scented.

Suitable companion plants for hostas in a white garden

For the type of white garden that selected hostas would enhance, the first requisite is some shade. In fact, many white-flowering plants would appreciate some protection from the hot afternoon sun. As the white area will most likely be just a part of the whole garden, perhaps a special border or bed, it will be necessary to use the shade from existing trees and shrubs.

If you don't have any existing shade, consider planting some smaller-growing trees. My first choice for this would be the spring-blooming white-flowered *Cornus florida* or flowering dogwood (zones 5–8): 'Eddie's White Wonder', 'Cloud 9' and 'Cherokee Princess' are old favorites. Other, more unusual candidates would be *C. controversa* 'Variegata', the wedding cake tree (zones 6–9), and perhaps the shrub-like *C. kousa*, which flowers in early summer instead of early spring. *C. k.* 'National', 'China Girl' or 'Milky Way' would all be excellent choices (zones 5–8).

These dogwoods would compose the 'top story' of a white garden. Beneath them some shrubs that have white flowers would be both desirable and suitable. Shrubs that bear scented flowers would give an extra dimension to the garden. If your climate is suitable for growing them, rhododendrons (including the evergreen azaleas) would provide these attributes.

Depending on the species or cultivar, hardiness zones for rhododendrons range from 4 to frost-tender. They are a very versatile group of plants and you are sure to find something that fulfils the size and color requirements of your garden. Any or all of the following would be splendid additions to a white garden: 'Albatross', 'Angelo', *Rhododendron decorum*, 'Loderi King George' and 'Polar Bear'. All these varieties are tall-growing specimens, which would suit underplanting. You could also consider the frost-tender *maddenii* series of rhododendrons, but only if your climate zone is 7 or over: *R. polyandrum* and *R. nuttallii* are two to look for.

Below the shrubs, the hostas and companion perennials will be planted. There are a great number of lovely white perennials that work well with hostas. You might consider planting Solomon's seal (*Polygonatum* spp.) (zones 3–9 depending on species), white dicentra (*Dicentra eximia* 'Alba') (zones 4–8), white astilbe (*Astilbe* 'White Gloria') (zones 4–8), any of the white hellebores (zones 4–9 depending on species), cultivars of *Convallaria majalis* (lily-of-the-valley) (zones 2–7), white cultivars of *Iris sibirica* (zones 4–9), and the lovely snowdrop *Galanthus nivalis* (zones 3–9). For further information on companion plants for hostas, see chapter 8.

Some companion plants for hostas in a white garden. From top: Solomon's seal; white astilbe, *Disporum variegatum*.

For a "hot" border

Borders devoted to flowers in bright colors are usually best situated in full sun, so hostas would not immediately spring to mind as being part of such a scheme. Why would one want hostas in a "hot" border anyway? Yet I have seen them used to divide one group of bright colors from another. Their soothing green leaves provide a wonderful contrast to the "hot" theme and create a more harmonious garden bed.

There are some hostas that can stand full sun, so all my suggestions here are for varieties with this ability. These large, sun-loving types will add extra color interest with their dramatic foliage.

A good blue called 'Blue Umbrellas' would be splendid as a divider, and its large, thick blue-green leaves are resistant to slug damage.

'Zounds' is a marvelous bright gold hosta with beautifully puckered leaves that would act as a complement for the yellow colors in a "hot" border. Unlike many other hostas, it does not change its color during the season and, I think, deserves to be used more widely.

'Invincible' has beautiful glossy dark green leaves with a unique texture that would look good among fiery colors. As a bonus, its white flowers are scented. It would work best at the front of a border because it is not very tall – about 14 in. by 10 in. (35 cm by 25 cm) – but if you have a suitable place, it is a most desirable plant.

'Francee' is so versatile that it puts itself forward for most situations, including here. It is green with white margins and finds sun quite acceptable.

In my opinion the most spectacular of the sun-lovers is the splendid 'Sum and Substance', which is large, with golden-chartreuse leaves that turn gold if grown in enough sun. Its leaves are very thick and have a smooth, matte appearance. This hosta is one of my all-time favorites and would look good in any situation.

OPPOSITE: H. fortunei 'Albopicta' (just before the bridge) works as a bright divider in a predominantly yellow border.

LEFT: Two suitable varieties for a sunny border are the blue 'Blue Umbrellas' and the green-gold 'Zounds'.

Perhaps the most spectacular of the sun-lovers is 'Sum and Substance'.

My next choice for the bright border is the species *H. plantaginea*, which revels in sun and, in fact, will not flower unless it has plenty of it. It would be a pity to miss out on the flowers, as it has the biggest of any hosta, and they are both white and scented. The form called 'Aphrodite' has scented double white flowers that are really wonderful. The pale green leaves are very pretty, and if only one variety were to be given a place in this border, *H. plantaginea* would be high on my list of favorites. A hybrid between *H. plantaginea* and *H. sieboldii* is called 'Honeybells'. As its name suggests, it is sweetly scented, likes sun and generally looks similar to *H. plantaginea*. Another hybrid is 'Royal Standard', which has all the virtues of its relations.

'Golden Sculpture' is quite new and very large, and is a pretty gold color with white flowers. It also likes sun and is resistant to snails, and its color does not fade during the season. What a grand addition this plant would make to any brightly colored border!

A splendid green hosta that will stand considerable sun is 'Green Fountain'. It has beautiful green leaves that cascade out from the bottom and arch just like a fountain.

The hostas mentioned here are all suitable for growing without shade, and thus would suit borders and beds which are sunny and full of bright color. Eventually, I hope more varieties will be bred that are sun-tolerant, but at present these are my best recommendations.

For a hosta walk

For those who feel they can never have too many hostas or who want a garden feature that will not require endless attention and maintenance, a hosta walk might be the answer. There are some famous hosta walks in both Britain and the United States, but their grandeur is beyond the scope of the average gardener. A hosta walk, however, does not have to stretch for a mile to be a very attractive addition to the garden.

What exactly is a hosta walk? Essentially it is a route or pathway through a garden delineated on each side by hostas. If you have a path or a driveway around the garden, and especially if it is partially shaded, you could create a special feature of it by turning it into a hosta walk.

A drive lined with trees or shrubs would be perfect for underplanting with hostas. But before you start throwing in any old hostas, it must be pointed out that a carefully thought-out plan will bring greater rewards.

A monochromatic scheme for a double walk

There are many combinations of hostas that would look good, but first let's consider a monochromatic scheme. If the drive is lined on both sides with trees, you could be very clever and ambitious and make a double walk. This means

A variety of hostas border a narrow paved walkway.

that each side will be an exact match of the other. For the color I would suggest using all shades of green, including light and lime greens. Depending on the length of the drive, you could plant in groups of either three or five.

At the back (remember this is being done on both sides) I would plant the splendid 'Guacamole', in my opinion one of the loveliest hostas. It has wonderful chartreuse leaves with wide dark green margins. It is large, so it needs plenty of space – leave about 3 ft. (90 cm) between plants. This might seem a little sparse in the beginning, but the gaps will fill in quickly because this plant grows vigorously. Still at the back, but moving up the drive, I would plant the popular 'Sum and Substance', whose puckered leaves are also chartreuse. This hosta is

A large garden path with a raised border of hostas as the main feature.

H. lancifolia is small enough to use alongside a narrow path bordering a house.

another that will grow to be very large and so the same spacing as for 'Guacamole' is necessary. To finish the background, try 'Snowden', a large, stately hosta that will look blue-green in the early spring, but will turn grayish-green later in the season. If you have a drive or entranceway longer than these three groups can fill, just repeat them. This strategy will provide some nice continuity.

Another possibility is to choose three medium-growing hostas in the green spectrum and alternate them. I recommend planting 'Invincible', with its shiny green leaves, followed by 'Krossa Regal', with its lovely vase-like shape, and finally the dark green puckered 'Sparkling Burgundy' all the way up the drive. I would finish off the planting by edging the whole route with the small green hosta 'Emerald Tiara'.

Bordering a narrow path

Paths, like drives, can be made into very attractive garden features when lined with different varieties of hostas. While you could very effectively use just one plant for this exercise, using more varieties and colors will result in greater visual interest and enjoyment. Many houses have paths to the front and back doors, along the sides of the house, and around the actual garden. A great many of these are starkly paved, but they can be softened by creating plant beds alongside them. This will give you an opportunity to use hostas, either by themselves or in conjunction with other perennials and shrubs. The places where the paths are not exposed to hot afternoon sun will be suitable sites for hostas.

As for which varieties and colors to choose, it really just depends on what you like. If the path and the bed beside it are narrow, smaller-growing 12 in. (30 cm) hostas would look best. If the bed is really narrow, it would probably look best when planted with one variety. If the bed is wider, then a mix would look lovely. For this sort of planting I think it is best to forget about groups and plant the hostas as individuals, either in blending colors or in a theme, such as gold.

Of course, a hosta walk does not need to be designed with any specific garden destination in mind. It may simply curve around existing features, or if the garden is being newly created or redesigned, it may be used to define specific areas.

Alongside a curved bed

If you are starting a new garden and set out a long, curving bed, you could plant the spine of the bed with trees and shrubs so that one side gets the morning sun and the other the afternoon blaze. On the shaded side that gets just the beneficial morning sun, you could plant a wonderful collection of hostas that follow the curve. (This is so much more appealing than a straight line, unless you prefer very formal plantings.) Here again you might consider planting groups of one variety or you could randomize the colors to make a tapestry of green, blue and gold, plus all sorts of variegated and margined hostas. If you like, the hostas could stand alone or you could use suitable companion plants (see chapter 8) alongside them. It depends on your taste and on how much space you have. If you have only one shady bed and it makes up most of your garden, you may want to use a greater variety of plants. If you have a very large garden (not so common these days) you might want to make the walk a real feature to display an extensive collection of hostas. (See chapter 5 for more on the use of hostas in small and large shaded gardens.)

In woodland gardens you have even more scope for creativity. The informal nature of these gardens provides possibilities for not only hosta-lined paths, but areas where a "surprise" might lurk in the form of a striking hosta specimen such as 'Great Expectations', 'On Stage', 'Striptease', 'Sagae' or 'Gold Standard'.

So, be it large or small, a hosta walk, either with just hostas, or with hostas and compatible plants, can add huge interest to a garden, and provide owners and visitors with a great deal of pleasure.

Hostas make an attractive feature around a curved bed.

Landscaping with Hostas: Some Typical Garden Settings

A large woodland-style garden

You've planted the trees for shade, thrown in some choice shrubs for interest, and chosen some wonderful plants for companions. The stage is set and the world's your oyster – in other words, you may now plant all and every hosta known to horticulture. That sounds wonderful, but most of us will be constrained by either space or budget, or both. Then again, "Rome was not built in a day" and your scheme might take a year or two to eventuate.

Establishing a new layout

Planting a large woodland-style garden is easier than planting a small one, which requires so much selection and planning. (See page 70 for ideas on landscaping smaller shade gardens.) The large garden will need to be divided, and one of the first things you need to think about is paths, which for this style of garden should, I think, meander informally rather than be rigidly straight. If you can make a path go around a corner, I find that you introduce an element of surprise and anticipation. If your shaded area is on a slope, as mine is, then you can divide it by having a path above, which gives you an overview, and another path through the middle, which will give you the opportunity to see more plants at close range.

OPPOSITE: **Hostas are the perfect plant for a woodland garden, where dappled shade and plenty of mulch keep them in peak condition.**

RIGHT: **'June' combines with** *Kalmia* **'Pink Charm' in this quiet woodland corner.**

Your next step is to form the paths and provide a safe walking surface. Concrete, asphalt, paving stones or brick are not suitable here, because a woodland-style garden should be informal. I favor shredded bark or wood chips, which soon fade to look natural and provide a secure footing. The material is not very expensive, and the paths can be topped up occasionally. Mown grass paths is another option.

With the planting areas defined, you can spray to kill the vegetation or, if poisonous sprays do not appeal, you can dig it all over. Woodland garden plants like an acidic, humus-rich soil, so adding manure would be ideal.

Planting up the beds

Now that the stage is set, it is a matter of deciding where to start. Once you have the paths in place, you will find that you have defined the beds. It is best to plant one bed at a time, so that each forms a separate segment of the whole. Some people like a complete plan before they start and others (like me) just plant as they go. For this particular hypothetical plan, I would plant the trees and shrubs a year or so in advance to provide shade, but if there is already shade provided, the understory planting can begin immediately. I would do this in the spring when the hostas are in leaf, because otherwise it can be difficult to visualize the overall picture. Of course, if you have a detailed plan you can plant even when the hostas are dormant.

As I have mentioned before, to create the most impact, it is best to plant in groups. Also, if you already have hostas, and you probably will have grown some or you would not be interested in a larger scheme, you can break these up (see chapter 3), which will give you a low-cost start. Once everything has been planted, a good thick mulch around the plants and over any exposed soil would be beneficial.

Some large blue hostas for background planting

For one planting scheme, I suggest filling the back of the bed with large blue hostas. These will create a stunning background and provide contrast for brighter-colored varieties in the foreground. Because there is more than one large blue hosta, you will have to make choices. You should not ignore the all-time favorite blue hosta, *H. sieboldiana* 'Elegans'. It is large, with heavily puckered, heart-shaped leaves and short, stout stems with white flowers, so a group of these in the background would be a great start to a garden bed. The next background group could be an *H. sieboldiana* form called 'Blue Angel', which is also very large, or possibly another form from the same parent called 'Big Daddy'.

Of course the planting is not going to be solely hostas, so now would be the time to plant some shade-loving perennials such as astilbes. Two or

'Big Daddy' is a large blue hosta suitable as a background plant.

three (or more) groups of three would look good. These could all be the same color, or they could be three different groups. *Astilbe* 'White Gloria' is fresh and bright, 'Fanal' is a most glorious red and 'Betsy Cuperus' is a graceful pink.

A golden contrast

Now, how about some color? As you have the space here and are planning to plant several beds, you need not cram everything into one area. Against such strong blues, golden hostas would look very attractive. Medium-sized plants would also be suitable here, so that the blue background is not obscured. I suggest 'August Moon', which, although it has been around since 1964, is still one of the best golds. It starts off green-gold, then turns, and stays, a very pleasing yellow. 'Birchwood Parky's Gold' is more modern and very pretty, while 'Glory' and 'Sun Power', planted in groups, would finish off this part of the planting nicely. To complement the gold hostas you could also plant yellow candelabra primulas. If you live in zone 6 or above, you could try the lovely *Primula helodoxa*. It is easy to grow, seeds nicely if suited to the site and flowers for a very long time. It is also scented.

The front row

To finish off this particular bed, small blue hostas could be used to great effect. Perhaps it would be fun to use some of Eric Smith's stunning small blues: 'Hadspen Blue', 'Hadspen Hawk', 'Hadspen Heron', 'Eric Smith' and the wonderful 'Halcyon' are all from his fabulous Tardiana group. Finally, I would scatter around plants of *Corydalis ochroleuca* (zones 6–8), which has green-tipped little white flowers. It is an enthusiastic spreader, but is also very easy to curb if you wish. I think it would lend an air of informality to the blue, gold and white planting.

A green and white tapestry

Although I have talked a great deal about planting in groups, the next bed I suggest is going to be different. Whatever design you choose, remember it does not have to be too rigid or conventional. The hostas in this bed are to be green with a white edge and planted at random. They are all of a medium size so that they don't obscure one another. The effect will look very striking. I suggest using more than one of a variety if you wish, but do not plant them together; rather, place them haphazardly throughout the bed.

First I would plant 'Decorata' because it is very pretty, costs little and is easily divided to provide more plants. *H. undulata* 'Albomarginata' could be described similarly. After that I would look to 'Pizzazz' with its very wide, white-margined leaves for drama. (The previous two mentioned have narrow

TOP: 'Sun Power'
ABOVE: 'Halcyon'

Three lovely green-and-white hostas for a woodland garden. From top: 'Grand Master', 'Sugar and Cream', 'Loyalist'.

margins.) Then I would follow with two ladies, 'Carol' and 'Mildred Seaver', and then the attention-grabbing 'Minuteman'. Next, the attractive and interesting *H. crispula*, which was introduced into Holland by Dr. von Siebold in 1829, and was one of the first hostas to reach Europe. It has an unusual twisted leaf and a white margin. It is nice to have a plant in your garden that can link the generations. 'So Sweet' is so named because its flowers are fragrant, but most gardeners select it for its looks alone. It has a very attractive habit of growth, a nicely rounded look, and although its edge begins creamy yellow, it turns white as the season progresses.

'Grand Master' carries on the colors, though perhaps its leaves have more white edge than green middle. The leaves are also long, pointed and truly striking. I don't know why 'Sugar and Cream' is so named, but it carries on the color scheme nicely. Next, just for fun, you could reverse the colors by using a white hosta with a green edge. You could do this using just one variety, 'Loyalist'. Although its color is loud, it is a very good accent plant to finish off the bed.

Consider using just one perennial as a companion, my all-time favorite *Polygonatum* species also known as Solomon's seal. There are a number of species and most have white flowers tipped with green. Choose one that suits your climate. They are delightful and easily grown plants.

A special hosta for a special place

I think you should always have something special happening in your garden, perhaps at the base of a statue or a tall tree. My favorite hosta deserves an important place where its beauty can be fully admired. This glorious plant is called 'Tokudama Aureonebulosa'. Its leaves are a mixture of cloudy gold, chartreuse and blue, with irregular blue-green margins. They are thick in texture and very corrugated. This description does not, of course, do this hosta justice. To keep it company, add some pink dicentra. I would choose a particularly pretty one, *Dicentra formosa* 'Langtrees' (zones 4–8), which has silver-gray leaves and pink-and-cream flowers. 'Tokudama Aureonebulosa' is slow growing and its color improves with age. Anyone who acquires it is really fortunate, hence its special and important place in the garden.

Some schemes featuring medio-variegated hostas

The term "medio-variegated" is new to me (these hostas are also described as "centrally marked") and I understand it is not approved, botanically speaking, but it is a useful term to describe hostas which have lighter leaf centers and darker margins. Some of my favorite hostas fall into this category, and they have already been introduced on page 47. I suggest featuring several of them in your large woodland-style garden.

A flashy grouping

Some of the medio-variegated hostas are subtle while others are very striking. The following types I call "flashy" and I suggest placing them in one of the shadier parts of your garden. Too deep a shade would not be suitable, but dappled shade in a spot that gets morning sun and little or no afternoon sun would be perfect. Here you could plant 'Fire and Ice' or the spectacular and eye-catching 'Patriot', which has wide white centers and narrow green edgings. The strangely named 'Night Before Christmas' shares the same coloring, but with a little less white and a little more green. My next choice would be 'Whirlwind', which is more colorful and has upright, pointed and twisted foliage with uneven white centers and dark green edges. The last in this flashy grouping is called 'Striptease', because between the green outside and yellow center is a narrow white strip. These four flashy hostas would look fantastic in groups of three or more.

As companions to these hostas I would plant *Aruncus dioicus* (goatsbeard) (zones 3–7), which is rather like a very large astilbe with fluffy white heads of flowers, or the pretty double white *Filipendula* 'Flore Pleno' (zones 3–9). To finish off, you could add some *Digitalis* species (foxgloves) (zones vary depending on species), preferably in white, although there are many other colors to choose from.

Some spectacular hostas that give real color and texture to a woodland planting.

TOP: 'Whirlwind'

LEFT: 'Patriot' in the foreground, with 'Sagae' and 'So Sweet' at the rear.

A trio in chartreuse

Next I suggest three more top hostas; they all have chartreuse-yellow centers, green-blue margins and heavily puckered leaves. They are a class act and would be some of my first purchases should I have to start again. 'Bright Lights' is much more subtle than its name suggests. It has a soft gold center and a streaky blue margin and makes a nice rounded clump. 'Lucy Vitols' is said to be one of the very best by the well-known American hybridizer Mildred Seaver. It is very puckered and rugose, and has chartreuse-green leaves with narrow blue-green margins. To round off this splendid trio I suggest 'September Sun', which has a lovely yellow center and green margin. Remember not to plant any of your hostas too close together – as they grow they increase in size considerably.

For companions you could add dainty columbines (*Aquilegia* spp.) in as many colors as you wish, because they will all blend beautifully. Another simple plant, the foamflower (*Tiarella* spp.), with its sprays of creamy white flowers, would also work well. I would plant *Epimedium* mostly for their leaves, which are nicely veined and change color with the seasons. The small flowers are also very pretty.

ABOVE: 'Spritzer'
RIGHT: 'Great Expectations'

Some eye-catching hostas for specimen planting

At a corner of a path it is fun to plant something unexpected. 'Spritzer' has long leaves with green margins and a bright yellow center. It is very eye-catching and suitable as a specimen plant. In the same color range is a really outstanding hosta called 'On Stage'. It grows fast and deserves a prominent place in the garden, just as its name suggests. Of course you could plant these in other places also, but as specimens they concentrate your attention on their attractions.

Thousands of people just love 'Great Expectations' and it has been a runaway favorite throughout North America. The only downside is that some gardeners have found it difficult to grow, which is unfortunate because it is arguably one of the most beautiful hostas ever bred and has grown very well for me. 'Great Expectations' has really beautiful large, puckered yellow leaves with wide, irregular margins of blue and green.

I would be inclined to plant something blue to contrast with the yellow in these hostas. You might consider common bluebells (*Hyacinthoides* spp., zones 4–9), which would make a nice carpet of color before the hostas wake. Although they can be invasive, they do not seem to worry hostas. *Brunnera macrophylla* (Siberian bugloss, zones 3–7) has flowers that are a lovely forget-me-not blue, and *Ajuga reptans* 'Jungle Beauty' has wonderful blue flowers and is taller than common *Ajuga* ground cover. With these companions in place, I would feel that I had paid due homage to this quite outstanding hosta.

There is a wonderful selection among medio-variegated hostas. I have a little statue of Salome (who looks very demure and does not have any sinful veils), which I have surrounded with 'June', which has gold leaves bordered with blue and green. Behind grows *Kalmia* 'Pink Charm' (zones 5–9) in beautiful pinky-red. I am pleased with this combination because 'June', which was the American Hosta Growers' top selection for 2001, is just stunning. I think this plant is essential in any good collection of hostas; its coloring looks quite sharp in the early spring and softens later in the season.

A few more subtle hostas

'Guacamole' is different from the other medio-variegated hostas mentioned because it is both larger in size and quieter in color. It has chartreuse-green leaves with a wide dark green edge. It grows large rather quickly, so it either has to be placed as a background or given lots of space if planted with others. I favor growing 'Guacamole' among another favorite called 'Paul's Glory'. In 1999 this hosta was the American Hosta Growers' Top of the Poll. 'Paul's Glory' has gold heart-shaped leaves with blue-green streaked edges and I am sure it will eventually be regarded as a classic. From their descriptions you might get the impression that many of these medio-variegated hostas are similar, but this is not so – they are all very different; their only sameness is that they are magnificent plants.

'Guacamole'

Companion plants need to be top quality for such lovely hostas, and I suggest the wonderfully tall, stately Himalayan lily *Cardiocrinum giganteum* (zones 7–9), with its scented cream flowers that are striped cinnamon red. To complete this aristocratic planting, you could bring in the handsome-leaved *Rodgersia aesculifolia* (zones 5–8), whose leaves resemble those of a horse chestnut. It also produces attractive spikes of white flowers.

There are a few more medio-variegated types that I would like to mention. First is the very popular 'Gold Standard'. It needs shade to be at its very best, and the leaves have bright gold centers with green margins. It mixes and matches well with other hostas. Next is a newer hosta called 'Super Nova', which has the same type of coloring but its leaves are a little cupped. The last in this very desirable group is called 'Inniswood', and while it has the same coloring, it still looks subtly different from the other two described.

Among this grouping you could plant hellebores (see chapter 8) so that these charming white, rose-pink, purple and wine-red flowers could take center stage while the hostas are still sleeping. Hellebores seed very freely, so make sure that they do not take over. Once they have been potted, the seedlings make good gifts for gardening friends (if they are patient and do not mind waiting a year or two for flowers).

More blue hostas for the larger garden

Blue hostas have always been popular. In fact, when hostas were not as common or as readily available as they are today, many people thought that a blue hosta, preferably with very large leaves, was the pinnacle of the genus. The choice is now so great that it would be very difficult to settle on just one, but nevertheless blue is still very popular, and quite deservedly so. On page 40 I introduced some of the classic blues for a mixed border. Here I want to suggest

BELOW: Two cup-shaped hostas with very different textures. 'Blue Arrow' left and 'Blue Blazes' right.

a group of medium-size modern blues of the highest standard and the bluest blue. This is no easy task, because there are so many now available, but, with difficulty, I have chosen six stunning medium blues, not necessarily in order of preference. 'Halcyon' is an exceptional blue that is particularly suited to a shade garden, where its color will appear more intense. 'Summer Haze' is not only a wonderful metallic blue, it also has thick, leathery leaves and a nice round habit of growth. 'Blue Arrow' is very well named because its pointed leaves reach upward, as do those of another modern hosta, 'Salute'. From Eric Smith, breeder of 'Halcyon', also comes another wonderfully intense color in 'Hadspen Blue'. To finish this distinctive group I would also include 'Blue Blazes', a new variety with cupped leaves.

As the companions for these blue beauties, you could plant the wonderful *Meconopsis grandis*, or Himalayan blue poppy (zones 5–8), which has the purest blue you could ever imagine in a flower. If it is really happy it will self-sow in your garden, but if this does not happen you will probably have to renew the plants every now and again, because these perennials are not long lived. However, they are truly worth any trouble.

The above planting appeals so much to me that, although I have it on a small scale, I think I will have to rearrange my garden to create more space in order to enlarge the scheme. My *Meconopsis* are happy, a situation that is not always easy to achieve, and the combination looks divine.

New and classic cream- and yellow-margined varieties

Hostas with cream or yellow margins are very attractive and there is now a large range from which to choose. The very top one is the absolutely splendid 'Sagae' (formerly called *H. fluctuans* 'Variegated'), which was Hosta of the Year in North America in 2000. Why so popular? Some

TOP: *Meconopsis grandis*, or the Himalayan blue poppy, looks very striking combined with hostas, but can be difficult to grow.
ABOVE: 'Sagae'

cynics say because it is so easily recognized, which is a real accomplishment considering that many other hostas look so much alike. Nobody would deny that 'Sagae' is the handsomest of plants, with its regal stance and frosted green vase-shaped leaves with creamy yellow edges. It is a sturdy plant that grows in beauty with the years and is best suited to a large shade garden where it can be given the generous space it needs.

To join 'Sagae' in the background, *H. montana* 'Aureomarginata' would be a good choice because it too is large and has an irregular yellow margin. The third plant in this trilogy could well be *H. ventricosa* 'Aureomarginata', which has the same general coloring, but with a twist at the end of the leaf.

'Tokudama Flavocircinalis'

Some medium growers

Among the medium growers there are plenty of choices. The hosta called 'Tokudama' has wonderfully puckered leaves, and I would suggest putting in 'Tokudama Flavocircinalis', which has heart-shaped blue-green and very substantial leaves with irregular gold margins. Next to this (or these if you have space for groups) could go another very popular hosta called 'Fragrant Bouquet', which is a soft green with a cream edge. Its flowers are sweetly fragrant, and it was top in the North American popularity poll in 1998.

In 1996 'So Sweet' was the popular choice. Its margins are cream turning to white, and it grows quite fast and has scented flowers. There is also the very fine 'Summer Fragrance', which also has a delightful perfume. I have always been fond of two very reliable and attractive hostas called 'Wide Brim' and 'Fringe Benefit'. They are both green with yellow margins and their names describe them well.

Three good edgers

I find the smaller-growing 'Sultana' delightful. With its wide margin, it has more character than many small plants. The leaves of 'Sultana' are both cupped and puckered; it is also a vigorous grower and so soon makes a sizeable clump.

The small-growing 'Sultana'.

'Anne Arett' is a favorite with most people, not only because it is attractive, but because it spreads very rapidly. This makes it ideal for edging, and it would look very attractive around the plants described above. This hosta has ruffled, lance-shaped leaves that are a pretty chartreuse with a cream edge. The chartreuse green turns darker during the summer and is a good alternative to 'Golden Tiara'. 'Bright Glow' is small, growing to only 1 ft. (30 cm). It is a dear little hosta and its golden leaves have a very pleasant heavy texture. It grows rapidly, has white flowers and is reportedly pest resistant.

For companions to these special hostas I think arisaemas in shades of green would look particularly good. Two that specifically come to mind are *Arisaema jacquemontii* (zones 7–9), which has white-striped light green spathes, and the hooded *A. triphyllum* (zones 4–9), which is also green. As a bonus, arisaemas produce bright red berries (seeds) that are often quite easily propagated.

Well, we have been through quite a large shade garden, planting dozens of choice hostas. I do not suppose for a minute that anyone will actually follow these plans to the letter, though I hope they might give you an idea or two, and will have informed you about some splendid plants.

Hostas thrive in a shady woodland environment.

TOP: A charming hosta planting with 'Jade Cascade' in the background and 'Great Expectations' and 'On Stage' providing the light green colors in the center.

ABOVE: Pulmonarias combine with 'Hadspen Blue' in a small raised bed.

A small shade garden

There are a great many more large shade gardens than small. This is probably because either the large garden has been designed specifically or a suitable canopy has been adapted. As for the small shade garden, any place where it is shady will do, and this is likely to be under a tree. If the tree is deciduous, the area beneath, with some treatment of the soil, could make a very successful little shade garden. The shade cast by a conifer, however, is too heavy and dark, and rain would have trouble penetrating.

If you have a silver birch, or even better, three silver birches in your garden, you could easily grow some hostas in their dappled shade. First you would need to consider the soil, because many trees are greedy for water and nutrients. You would need to enrich the soil with humus, well-rotted manure and a mulch. While that takes care of the soil structure, to successfully grow hostas, water is also necessary. Your particular climate might kindly provide you with enough moisture, but if it does not, there are small affordable watering systems that are very effective. If you want a little more sophistication you could try a timing device that will automatically water your plants on a designated day for a designated time.

If your garden is small you will not wish it to have just one type of plant. You will therefore need to choose companion plants and hosta varieties with great care so that the plants are not only harmonious and in proportion, but offer interest, in either flower or foliage, for most of the year.

Hostas are, of course, grown mainly for their foliage, but they also have flowers. These come in shades of lavender, purple or white, and so would fit into most color schemes. When creating a little shade garden it would be foolish to grow great big showy hostas like 'Great Expectations', so we will concentrate on medium or small-growing types and will not plant them in groups, which might overwhelm any companion planting.

A blue and white bed around birches

If you prefer, you could concentrate on only one or two colors for the bed. I suggest blue and white. We will start by choosing hostas that are a really definite blue and of a medium or small size. (Do not be alarmed if late in the season your blue hostas turn green; this is perfectly normal.)

Any from Eric Smith's Tardiana group would be ideal. Among the lovely blue Tardiana hostas I suggest planting spring-flowering bulbs, because they use the light before the leaves appear on the trees, and afterwards mingle quietly into the general scheme. For late winter–early spring you could grow the lovely little snowdrop called *Galanthus nivalis* (zones 3–9), which has a green-tipped slender white flower. All snowdrops look very much the same, with nodding white flowers and a green mark on the top of each inner petal, so it won't make much difference which variety you choose. However, keep in mind that the smaller-growing varieties have smaller leaves that won't dominate the other plants once the flowers are over.

Erythronium are very generous because their leaves as well as their flowers are beautiful. *E. californicum* 'White Beauty' (zones 3–9) is ideal because its light green leaves are mottled and the petals of its pendant white flowers are reflexed, and reveal a pretty brown ring near the center of the flower. These delightful spring bulbs increase very easily. Another spring treasure for the blue and white shade garden is *Cyclamen coum* 'Album' (zones 5–9). I have never known anyone who could resist a cyclamen flower, and this one is just gorgeous. It has white flowers that sport a distinctive maroon mark at the mouth. The leaves of *C. coum* are deep green and rounded, sometimes with silver patterns.

During the summer the hosta leaves will carry the garden through, and some will add their colorful flowers to the overall show. Come fall the hostas are getting past their best, so you could feature *Cyclamen hederifolium* var. 'Album' (zones 7–9), which has pure white flowers and the most astonishingly beautiful ivy-shaped leaves that are patterned in silver.

There is also *Colchicum speciosum* 'Album' (zones 4–9), often known as a fall crocus. Fall is correct, crocus is not, but this little beauty has cup-shaped white flowers that do indeed look like a crocus.

Once winter comes, it is time to tidy up the bed and cover it with a good blanket of mulch, until it's time to start all over again in the spring.

An ideal companion plant for the small shade garden is the lovely *Cyclamen coum* 'Album'.

A medio-variegated hosta bed under maples

Assuming for now that your small garden also rejoices in one or more Japanese maples, here is a plan to underplant these with hostas. Having enriched the soil and provided moisture if necessary, you could choose medio-variegated hostas. I think they are particularly beautiful, and often give them blue-flowered bulbs or perennials for companionship. As usual, for this particular planting you need to be careful not to choose plants that will get too big – nothing over about 18 in. (45 cm).

In 2001 'June' was the American Hosta Growers' selection for Hosta of the Year and anyone seeing it can appreciate why it received this honor. It is actually a sport of 'Halcyon'. 'June' has gold leaves bordered by blue and green. The leaves are very bright early in the season but gradually soften as the year goes on. Although I have said that small shade gardens should not have plantings in groups, I would like to make an exception. I propose to use the hosta 'Tokudama Aureonebulosa' in a planting of three. It has heavily textured leaves that are streaked chartreuse yellow, with blue-green edges.

Among these beauties could be scattered bulbs of the lovely little *Chionodoxa* (zones vary according to species), which has upward-facing blue flowers with a white eye. You could add *Crocus tommasinianus* (zones 3–8), a pretty early-flowering bulb with lavender-blue flowers, which spreads happily. A plant does not have to be rare to be beautiful, so some *Muscari* (grape hyacinths, zones vary according to species) would look attractive with their spikes of blue flowers. They will undoubtedly spread and you can always relocate, give away or discard what you consider surplus to requirements.

An attractive perennial to enhance this scheme would be *Brunnera macrophylla* 'Dawson's White' (zones 3–7), which has green heart-shaped leaves with a broad white margin and tiny blue flowers.

Meconopsis species, the Himalayan poppies, can be a little fussy about its environment, but is worth trying because of its astonishing beauty. You could treat it as an annual and grow it from seed each year.

Fritillaria pallidiflora has wonderful greenish yellow flowers delicate enough for the smallest of gardens.

We will finish this scheme by planting *Ajuga reptans* 'Atropurpurea' (bugle-weed, zones 3–9), a ground cover with dark purple leaves and spikes of blue flowers that will provide interest for most of the year. It will undoubtedly spread, but is easily enough weeded out.

A little gold and yellow garden

I would like to propose one more planting scheme, this time featuring small to medium yellow and gold hostas. I suggest starting with 'Glory', which has bright yellow heart-shaped leaves that remain the same color throughout the season. I would team it with an equally desirable hosta called 'Sun Power', which has the reputation of being one of the very best golds. Joining this elite group could be 'Zounds', a beautifully puckered plant with metallic bright gold leaves. To the bed I would next add three slightly smaller gold hostas: 'Golden Medallion', 'Golden Prayers' and 'Golden Scepter'.

If some small-growing yellow bulbs are required for this area, the first to come to mind are *Narcissus* (daffodils, zones vary depending on cultivar but generally range from 3–9). Choose small-growing varieties so as not to have too many leaves overshadowing other plants. *N. jonquillia* (wild jonquils) and *N. cyclamineus* would also suit the garden beautifully. *N. cyclamineus* daffodils have lovely pendulous flowers with a long reflexed trumpet in a beautiful bright gold. The scented jonquils are popular too, because they flower so early in the spring. 'Baby Moon', with soft yellow scented blooms, is an excellent variety.

Fritillaria are special plants and there is none more beautiful than *F. pallidiflora* (zones 5–8), which has rather nice lance-shaped gray-green leaves and heavenly greenish yellow flowers. Bell-shaped and nodding, they are faintly checkered brownish red inside, and if you are not already familiar with them, you will certainly be enchanted when they flower. If you want to plant *Erythronium* for this garden, I suggest the variety 'Pagoda', which has nicely mottled leaves and pretty pale yellow flowers. It has the virtue of having multiple flowers on each stem.

A formal garden with hostas as part of the central square beds.

Formal gardens

A formal garden design uses space in straight lines, or in squares, oblongs or triangles. Often the whole garden is enclosed with meticulously clipped hedges that provide shade at their bases for hostas. When straight lines are required, groups of threes or fives would not be suitable; in this situation hostas must be placed very formally. For example, lines of one variety might be planted spanning the whole length of a hedge. If the space is wide enough, multiple lines can be planted, using one variety for each line, but not necessarily the same variety as the first planting. Varieties that blend harmoniously would be most appropriate, rather than the more spectacularly colored kinds.

Often the long, straight planting described can be mirrored by using exactly the same design on an opposite bed that is separated by mown grass or paving. This formality can have a very soothing, calming effect, because there is nothing spontaneous in the design. These days formality is often tempered by a planting that allows plants to behave informally by spilling over edges. Sometimes the individual gardens enclosed in the overall formal garden are quite small, and often small-growing, more sun-tolerant hostas like 'Ginko Craig' are good choices. 'Ginko Craig' has green lance-shaped leaves with bright white margins. *H. undulata* has this coloring reversed – it has creamy white leaves with narrow dark green margins and it is a very easy hosta to grow.

Good hosta edgers for the formal garden

For edging in a formal garden (or, for that matter, an informal garden) 'Blue Cadet' is very good. It has pretty blue-green leaves, is low growing and has very attractive pale lavender flowers. In a light lemon to chartreuse color is another very pretty little edger called 'Lemon Lime'.

Another superb choice for edging is *H. tardiflora*, whose name means late flowering. It is useful in a hosta bed when all other hostas have finished. It also flowers prolifically. It has lance-shaped leaves of a lustrous dark green and grows to about 10 in. (25 cm). As an added bonus, snails do not seem to care for its flavor.

If you have visited a garden that grows a lot of hostas, you probably will have seen my next choice for edging, *H. lancifolia*. Introduced into Europe by the famous von Siebold in 1829, this useful little edging plant grows up to 1 ft. (30 cm) and is both slender and elegant. It has good dark olive-green leaves and purple flowers on tall scapes.

Should little gold hostas seem appropriate, 'Golden Scepter' is an attractive all-gold form of 'Golden Tiara'. 'Gold Drop' and 'Good as Gold' would create a very pretty trio.

Although there is not enormous scope for hosta planting in the beds and borders of formal gardens (unless they can be given a reasonable amount of shade), there is still a place for some of these very versatile plants. They can also excel as specimen plants for urns and other containers used in formal gardens, or for enhancement of certain special features in such designs. (See chapters 6 and 7 for examples.)

FAR LEFT: A large hosta provides dramatic foliage in this formal bed.

LEFT: A good small-growing edger for a formal garden is the neat and compact 'Blue Cadet'.

A small city or retirement garden

Friends who have moved from larger gardens to a smaller area tell me that it is much more difficult to plant in a smaller space. It is a real design challenge, and the key word for small-space gardeners is "selection." Even the smallest gardens often have shady areas that provide a promising environment for hostas. For example, on the shaded side of the house a mass planting of hostas makes a very effective display and needs minimum care. Be sure, however, to choose hostas that will not outgrow a relatively narrow space.

If your aim is to brighten up a shady area, the first hosta that comes to mind is the delightful and very pretty 'Golden Tiara'. It grows to about 12 in. (30 cm) and increases very rapidly. It has soft green heart-shaped leaves with a gold margin, and looks particularly good when planted in groups. 'Chinese Sunrise' is another small-growing hosta that has a chartreuse-gold center and a narrow green margin. During the summer the center fades to a dull green.

'Ginko Craig' is about the same size, but it has a dark green leaf bordered with an irregular white margin. A little more striking is 'Celebration', which has lance-shaped cream leaves with green margins. 'Blond Elf', which is a subtle gold, makes a nice neat mound, while 'Inaho' has pointed yellow leaves with green streaks all through them. I have not seen this one planted in any large groupings but think it would look very striking.

One more hosta for this shady border is 'Vanilla Cream'. It is quite small at 3 in. by 8 in. (8 cm by 20 cm) and starts out light green, then turns chartreuse, then gold and finally cream. This one gives you a lot of hosta for the price of one!

Medium growers for limited space

Apart from their use in borders, the rest of the small garden hostas are best when they take a supporting role among other perennials. Once again, the really large hostas (those growing over 3 ft. or 1 m) would not be very appropriate, but there are many other lovely medium growers in both plain and fancy styles. If the space is very limited and you want a selection of hostas, forego planting in groups and have just one of each variety.

I will recommend just six medium growers, none of which are above 2 ft. (60 cm). The first is a stunning blue hosta that has not been available until recently. It is called 'Salute' and its leaves are pointed and stand upright. 'Maya Gold' is another pretty choice and is lime green–gold. Still in this combination but much brighter is the new 'Midwest Magic', which has gold, green-margined leaves. For something brisk and bright try 'Minuteman', which has a dark green center with a very striking wide white margin. 'Green Wedge Klehm' is also a very pleasant green hosta for the garden. Finally, for my last suggestion I propose a scented green variety called 'Flower Power'.

If you have a very small garden, growing hostas in containers is another option (see chapter 7).

Three medium-growing hostas suitable for a smaller garden.
ABOVE LEFT: 'Maya Gold'
ABOVE CENTER: 'Salute'
ABOVE RIGHT: 'Minuteman' in a container.

Courtyard gardens

Courtyards are paved spaces enclosed by walls or fences, which may cast shade throughout the day. Usually there are perimeter plantings of trees and shrubs between which are ideal spots for shade-loving plants such as hostas. There are, naturally, many ways to decorate your courtyard; the following are just a few suggestions to help in your selection process. Always keep in mind that a garden is an individual creation. The important thing is that the finished project pleases you and reflects your taste. Books are useful only in telling you how to grow plants, letting you know what is available and what to expect of your chosen plants; the rest is up to you.

Some trees ideal for a courtyard

For the perimeter trees I would use *Acer palmatum*, the Japanese maple (zones 6–8). Not only are maples outstandingly beautiful, but, chosen carefully, they will not grow too large. Among smaller-growing trees *Cornus* species (dogwoods) could also take a prominent place, and together these two trees would make a splendid background.

Of course all *Acer palmatum* are not the same size, so it would be sensible to choose moderate growers, and fortunately this will not restrict your choice too drastically. I would list *A. p.* 'Katsura', 'Shin-deshojo', 'Beni-otake', 'Beni-komachi' and 'Osakazuki' all for their outstanding fall color as well as lovely new growth each spring. *A. p.* 'Seiryu' is very dainty, with finely dissected green leaves that turn a strong gold, often suffused crimson, in fall. *A. p.* 'Villa Taranto' I consider a real treasure because its green leaves are overlaid with a delicate soft red.

I love all Japanese maples and there are many more to choose from. A visit to your garden center in the spring would demonstrate their beauty to you. There are also lovely weeping Japanese maples, which have a part to play in the courtyard, but not as shade trees – they act more as accent plants, and they look wonderful in pots on the paving.

TOP: The large, rounded leaves of the hostas contrast nicely with the other foliage in this small courtyard corner.

ABOVE: Multicolored hostas create a dense, lush border. The blues, greens and gold work well with the courtyard's paving.

In addition to perimeter beds, courtyards sometimes have a center bed. If the courtyard is of a reasonable size it would look absolutely spectacular if a *Cornus controversa* 'Variegata' (zones 6–9) were planted as the main feature. This splendid tree is often called the "wedding cake tree" because its branches grow in layers or tiers. It has green leaves margined white and is quite special.

The only other small tree that I shall mention for the courtyard is the lovely *Cercis canadensis* 'Forest Pansy', a variety of eastern redbud (zones 5–9). It has outstanding large wine-red heart-shaped leaves that turn shades of orange and tan in the fall. If I had to settle for only three types of deciduous tree, 'Forest Pansy' would join the Japanese maple and magnolia as my choices.

Having planted the courtyard trees at proper spaces, there will be room for some shrubs as a second tier. If your climate zone is around 7 or 8, choose camellias, with their attractive shiny foliage and wonderful range of flower colors and sizes. If you are in a cooler climate, you might like to consider growing a specimen or two in containers. For climates down to zone 5, the Mollis azaleas (*Rhododendron molle* subsp. *japonicum*) can provide scented flowers in a kaleidoscope of brilliant fall colors.

Two medio-variegated hostas with subtle leaf color for a small courtyard planting. *TOP:* 'Rascal' *ABOVE:* 'Bright Lights'

Medio-variegated hostas in subtle shades

As already described (see page 47), medio-variegated hostas are very bright and dramatic; however, for my first planting scheme for the courtyard I would use varieties in more subtle colors. For most, the colors start softly then change during the season into brighter and more definitive patterns. I must confess, however, that I prefer the softer early season colors, although the later change of color is wonderful too. It is like having two plants in one.

If your courtyard is small you might like to use just one variety in repeating groups. Your only difficulty will be in deciding which one to choose. I would use 'Lucy Vitols', not only because of its coloring, which is a pale yellow-green center with a narrow darker green margin (the center turns a lovely bright gold later), but because the leaves are very puckered.

If you want to add another hosta that would blend nicely with 'Lucy Vitols', choose the lovely 'Bright Lights', which has thick, heart-shaped leaves. These are also puckered and the centers are a soft gold with a streaky blue margin. Later the pale gold turns a more intense color and the blue edge changes to green.

If your courtyard is larger and you would like to use more varieties, I would recommend 'September Sun', a very beautiful sport of 'August Moon'. It has pale yellow leaves, margined green, that retain their soft colors all season.

You might also want to consider a very new hosta called 'Rascal'. It has soft, pale lemon-yellow leaves that are edged in pale green. It goes albescent (i.e., white) later in the season.

6 Landscaping with Hostas: Enhancing a Garden's Special Features

Integrating strong focal points

In many gardens there is a focal point, very often a statue, sundial, pergola, seat, stones or other ornaments. These special features should not stand out starkly; they need a planting to soften them and to help integrate them into the garden. Hostas play an important part here, because their beautiful and often very large leaves are excellent for hiding the base of a decorative structure or object. Conversely, these versatile plants can also help to spotlight the features in certain areas where they might otherwise be overlooked.

I have a fondness for stones and I often plant hostas next to them so in the winter, when the hosta has disappeared, the stone can display its beautiful shape and form. I have 'Chinese Sunrise' planted next to a stone in my garden and it looks very much at home. Since the stone is quite large and the hosta is

OPPOSITE: A charming garden statue surrounded by lush hostas and companion plants.

RIGHT: A wishing well and hostas.

FAR RIGHT: The light margins of 'Decorata' complement the lichen-covered trunk in this secret garden corner.

Raised beds, interesting pots and garden seats can all be enhanced by a well-placed hosta planting.

quite small, it forms a pleasing composition. There are other stones scattered through this planting in my garden and they can get smothered by the hostas in the summer, but they always look good during the winter months and during the fall when they are draped with the yellow leaves of the departing hostas.

There are many garden statues out there to choose from. Although these statues may seem expensive, remember that they are permanent. It pays to select such an item carefully. From experience, I can tell you that in the long run, it is never sensible to buy something you do not like just because it is cheaper. In my shade garden I have a statue of two children sheltered under an umbrella and surrounding it is a mixed planting featuring hostas and *Dicentra* species. This statue actually sits on the base of a tree that fell in a storm, which brings us to another consideration. Usually, unless they are very tall, statues need to be raised on a tree stump, a plinth or some other base; otherwise they are liable to be swamped. If this happens you have lost the whole point of having a statue because it will no longer be a focal point.

In the past, I have placed a tall pot of hostas in the garden to create a vertical feature, and have surrounded the base with a planting of hostas.

Pergolas usually have a shaded side, so a few pots of hostas can add a great deal of interest at the ground level, while the clematis or roses, or whatever you have chosen as a climber, can show off higher up.

Seats can be most ornamental and often provide an endpoint to a vista. Seats, of course, do not have to sit in lonely splendor, but can have hostas around the base, and preferably a tree behind to provide shade for both plant and person.

I have a friend who made a charming wishing well for his garden with a shingled roof and gave it a background of hostas. If you can, try to use enhancements in your garden and remember to soften them with a planting of hostas.

Hostas for water features

Hostas and water go together very well. Although hostas can tolerate various degrees of sun, they cannot abide being dry. Planting them next to streams, ponds or waterfalls helps them to stay moist and creates a splendid visual picture in your garden. Water features can range from a basin to a birdbath, fountain, pond, stream or lake, and all can be enhanced by the addition of hostas. If your water is just a little basin, as frequently seen in Japanese gardens, you might be restricted to one carefully chosen hosta, but fortunately many gardeners can manage a little more than this. At the other end of the scale would be a lake with an extensive perimeter planting and enough trees and shrubs to provide shade from the hot afternoon sun. A really impressive landscape could be achieved by using all the medium- and taller-growing hostas that you fancied, or by planting great swaths of one variety.

Plants for a pond

For most gardeners a pond is a more realistic option than the large lake planting mentioned above. If you are putting in a new pond, site it where it will have at least dappled shade in the afternoon. If your pond is already in existence, you may need to create this dappled shade with plantings of trees and shrubs. This shade will enable some really good specimen hostas to be planted around the pond, among other plants or just by themselves.

The size of the hostas you choose to plant should always be in proportion to the size of the pond. For a medium-sized pond, say over 6 ft. (1.8 m) in diameter, there is a huge choice of hostas, depending on your taste. Green hostas always look good in this setting, and green leaves with a white edge,

Hostas edging a large pond.

or white variegation, create a crisp effect. You might also consider trying something really dramatic and brightly colored. I will name a few medium growers in these categories to help with your selection.

For a medium-sized green hosta, I recommend 'Green Fountain', which has a graceful, cascading habit, *H. ventricosa*, which has both poise and shape, or *H. plantaginea* 'Aphrodite', which has the advantage of white scented flowers. If you are looking for a dramatic green-and-white hosta (dramatic because the white margins on its leaves are very wide) try 'Patriot'. Even more eye-catching are 'Fire and Ice' and 'Night Before Christmas', which have wide white centers and green edges.

In the dramatic brightly colored category you could not do better than the widely acclaimed 'Great Expectations', arguably one of the most beautiful hostas of all. It has puckered yellow leaves with wide, irregular margins of blue and light green. Another that would work well with this grouping is 'Paul's Glory', which was the American Hostas Growers' selection for Hosta of the Year 1999. It has gold heart-shaped leaves bordered by a blue-green streaked margin, and it would look very nice next to 'Great Expectations'.

Stream-side hostas

If you are fortunate enough to have a stream running through your garden, you have a wonderful natural environment for hostas. Stream edges are always damp and because of this the hostas planted here will be able to tolerate more sun, though as usual, some afternoon shading would still be ideal. The most attractive way to create a stream-side planting is by using groups of one variety in varying heights and colors. Make sure you do not plant tall hostas too close together, as they will form a "hedge" and you will not be able to see the water. Planting groups wide apart rather than running a border along the bank always looks very natural and is visually pleasing.

A fountain highlight

A fountain is a lovely thing and, once again, provides a wonderful place for a hosta or two. Sometimes less is more, and using just one particularly beautiful hosta looks both stunning and unfussy. I suggest the wonderful blue 'Salute', which stands upright at attention, or maybe the extraordinary 'Whirlwind', with its upright twisted and pointed leaves, their dark green margins enhancing the greenish cream centers.

I hope my suggestions will help you see that ornamental water features are a great blessing in the garden and can always be wonderfully enhanced by the planting of hostas nearby.

OPPOSITE: A beautiful stream-side planting featuring hostas, including *H. undulata, H. montana, H. sieboldiana* and 'Decorata'.
TOP: 'Wide Brim'
ABOVE: Variegated hostas surround a small fountain.

Growing Hostas in Containers

Lately I have become very interested in growing hostas in pots, which has rather surprised me because I have a very large garden and grow literally hundreds of these plants. However, if you have hostas in containers near the house you have the opportunity to observe each variety closely – much more so than you do when they are planted in a large area. Also, the need for frequent watering means you pay more attention to the plants. Container gardening is a skill that can be developed with practice. There is more to it than just placing a plant in the pot and then watering it. It is necessary to display the container and the hosta or hostas to full advantage. Although a single specimen can be used as a focal point, more often than not a group of plants will make a more pleasing composition. To do this you will need containers and hostas of various sizes.

Why grow plants in containers?

Pots of hostas can add great interest to shaded decks, patios and other areas near the house, particularly where paving prohibits planting. A strategically placed container can make a feature, or a group can be used to screen something that you do not want to see. In the garden itself, particularly in the mixed border, sometimes gaps appear that were not in your plan when you started it. When this happens, do what the great English gardener Gertrude Jekyll used to do and pop in a pot. If the other vegetation will not cover the pot, dig a hole and bury the container. Sometimes if your garden has mature trees, you will find that roots prevent you from planting anything under them. This is another place where you can put potted hostas.

Container gardening provides immediate impact and is easy to do. It is also great if you live in a small apartment or retirement home where there is very little space for gardening. Any area that has paved, graveled or concrete areas is ideal for containerized plants. It is a consolation to the dedicated gardener of advancing years who has moved to a small place and is still able to grow plants. Even those whose mobility is not so good can tend to pots without much outside help. Container planting allows people to retain some of their gardening independence.

Choosing suitable containers

If you are planning to grow hostas in pots, you will need, to paraphrase Mrs. Beeton, to "first catch your container." There is a wide variety of pots available for a wide range of prices. I greatly favor terracotta pots, but hand-made pots are also wonderful. There are many brightly colored and patterned terracotta pots on the market and you could have a lot of fun color coordinating your collection. I would not recommend plastic pots, not only for their appearance

OPPOSITE: This moss-covered urn containing 'Pizzazz' provides a brilliant focal point in a sea of lush hosta leaves.

Matching the hosta to the container is half the fun: relative size, color and shape all play a part.

but because they do not breathe, which is bad for all but short-term plants like annuals. Wooden containers look natural and will last for quite a long time, and stone or concrete containers can be unsuitable because of their weight, but could be considered if they are to be placed in a permanent position.

Fewer but larger pots will make the most visual impact when you are container planting. Larger pots also require less watering than smaller ones. I have measured my pots and they range from about 16 in. (40 cm) in diameter to 2 ft. (60 cm). The height of these pots is between 12 in. and 16 in. (30 cm and 40 cm). I greatly favor Italian-made terracotta pots, which are of excellent quality and do not break easily. After a few years I have found that some of the cheaper containers will crack, or their rims will peel off.

Planting up your containers

Your pot must have drainage holes. To keep them from getting blocked, place pieces of broken pots or some stones in the bottom of the container. After that, add a layer of gravel to ensure that drainage is free-flowing so the plant does not get waterlogged, which would cause it to die. Fill your container with potting mix and add some slow-release fertilizer. Before placing the plant, it is helpful to water the mix in order to settle it down, and then top it up with a bit more potting mix. From experience I have found that if you do not do this you end up with a plant that sits well below the top of the container.

Now it is time for you to plant the hosta. If the hosta comes out of a bag or pot, tease its roots so that they come free and can start to move out into the mix. Water well after planting. Once the plant has started to grow strongly, I like to add a layer of well-rotted manure to the top of the mix. If you do not have manure, compost also works well. If you wish, you could also occasionally give your plant a foliar feed. Other than watering when needed, which may be as often as once a day in the summer months, you do not have to fuss with the plants. Weeds are not usually a problem because the hosta's leaves will shade them out.

You probably have a good idea of where you want to place your pots, but before you make your decision have a good look at what will be behind the containers so that you do not have colors that clash between plant and wall. I think that with most hostas this would not be a major problem, but a yellow-brick wall would not do much for a gold hosta. I have white-painted walls and I find them too harsh as a backdrop for my hostas. Generally, however, it is not too difficult to create pleasing compositions.

Container gardening in cold climates

Just as hostas in the garden require attention every so often, so do container-grown hostas. I've already mentioned the need for regular watering and feeding, but for people who live in cooler climates there is an additional concern come winter. If you don't suffer heavy frosts or snow during winter you will probably only have to tidy up the plants as they die back, and water them occasionally during winter. But for everyone else it is necessary to take more affirmative action – unless you want to treat your hostas as annuals.

As the temperature falls and the plants die back, remove the spent flower scapes and leaves, then move the pots to a shed, garage or even a sheltered porch where the temperature will stay relatively constant and not drop too far below freezing point. An even temperature will prevent the plant from trying to grow out of season. Don't let the pots experience a hard freeze-thaw cycle either; not only will you damage the plant, but you may also end up with cracked and broken pots. Water the containers lightly through the winter – you don't want the soil to dry out completely.

Hostas in containers are less insulated from temperature shifts than plants in the garden, so they will usually shoot up earlier. Don't be fooled into thinking it is safe to place them outside just because they have started to grow – wait until the danger of hard frosts has passed; otherwise you will lose your carefully saved plants. If your pots are too heavy to bring indoors, you might like to try burying your plants in the garden and repotting them come spring.

Positioning your pots

Pots look best in a variety of ways. You can place them in groups of the same type, or create a composition with different-sized containers and different varieties of hostas, or you can simply use one pot as a focal point. At this exciting stage of planning it is essential to remember that it is hostas that you are planting and not daisies, and so it will be necessary to choose places that do not get afternoon sun. Morning sun is perfectly acceptable; in fact, if they do not get some sun the plants will look unwell and will certainly not flower.

For special occasions you can move your plants temporarily to enhance the backyard area or add charisma to the site of a family photo. It is handy to have some sort of low-wheeled trolley or wagon to help you move the pots and to guard against giving yourself a hernia. During the season you may decide to move pots to change their composition or to shift them when the summer-high sun searches out a spot that was shaded in the spring. Unless you have a strong, sturdy (and preferably young) man in residence, a trolley is essential.

Container creativity

The really interesting part of container planting is when considering design, form, balance and color. Creating balance is not difficult; it merely involves shifting things around until they please the eye. Design involves working out which pots will suit which plants and then deciding whether to place them in large groups or simply in groups of twos or threes. Form concerns the kind of plant and its habit in relation to the size and shape of the container.

Arranging your containers is a skill that will improve as you experiment. Of course this is one of the great virtues of container gardening – you can change the whole concept at the trundle of a trolley. For many of us it is not easy to see the finished result in the mind's eye. In container gardening if you've made a design error, don't worry – just start moving things around.

Almost every building has suitable places for pots. Most houses have an area of hard landscaping such as gravel, concrete, paving, etc., that can be used. You can also place containers near entrances, paths, steps and walls. These places are your canvas and you should enhance them as it suits you. If the space is quite large, such as in a paved area, a group of pots would be suitable. Keep in mind that uneven numbers look most natural. I think that in a larger space a group of pots in different sizes and with different varieties of hosta looks best. You might like to choose all one color but in different varieties, or you could mix and match, which could be more exciting.

There is often a path on the shady side of the house that could be greatly enhanced with pots. You could also put your containers near steps, front

'Guacamole' on the left and 'Striptease' on the right.

doors (if shaded by a porch), back doors, verandas, the bases of pergolas (if shaded by an overhead planting) and the bases of walls. If you have a garden that is partly shaded you could use a tall pot or urn (or raise the pot by providing a base) to create a stunning vertical accent.

A scheme for seven pots

I usually plant a single hosta in each pot, but everyone has different ideas and, if your container is big enough, you might like to plant more than one hosta or to add some companion plants. For a larger area where seven containers could fit comfortably, I recommend a mix that includes both blue and green as a contrast to brighter colors. Pots of about 16–20 in. (40–50 cm) in diameter are large enough for medium-sized hostas. For the greens, you could plant *H. ventricosa*, which has dark green leaves, and pair it with the lighter-colored 'Green Wedge Klehm'. For the blues I would choose 'Salute', with its pointed, upstanding leaves, and 'Summer Haze', whose foliage is glaucous blue, thick and puckered. Lastly, I would select three medio-variegated plants, including 'Lucy Vitols', which has very heavily puckered yellow-green leaves with a narrow green band; 'Bright Lights', with heart-shaped gold leaves margined in a streaky blue; and my all-time favorite, 'Tokudama Aureonebulosa', which has cup-shaped, heavily textured yellow leaves with striking deep blue margins.

A potted collection of young hostas.

A potted collection of small-growing hostas

If you wanted a planting of smaller varieties you could put together a collection of the Tiaras, which are small, clump-forming hostas. The best known are, 'Golden Tiara', which is mid-green with a well defined yellow margin; 'Diamond Tiara', which has a white margin; 'Emerald Tiara', which is gold with a green margin; and 'Grand Tiara', which has a wider bright gold margin and a narrow green center. These plants do not grow above about 12 in. (30 cm), so they would not need a huge pot. In my opinion they look best as a separate group, but of course they could make a foreground planting around larger pots.

I have mentioned Eric Smith's Tardiana group frequently in this book and that is because his hostas are so beautiful and unbelievably blue. While I have them in my garden, this coming season I plan to have a collection in pots. I am planning to arrange them something like this: the magnificent 'Halcyon' will be the centerpiece since it is taller at 20 in. (50 cm) than the others, and around it I will cluster 'Hadspen Blue', 'Hadspen Heron', 'Dorset Blue' and 'Hadspen Hawk' (see chapter 9). This collection will be placed in a very choice spot and will be studied with pleasure.

As I have described earlier, hostas go through stages from spring to fall. Each stage is interesting and is probably most easily observed in potted specimens. The stunning shoots, sometimes blue or green, green and white, or green flushed pink, are the first delight. Next are the unfolding leaves, which are plain or puckered and come in a spectrum of colors. Then there are the flowers in lavender, purple or white. In the fall the leaves turn golden and, after a break for winter, the endless cycle of the seasons starts again.

A group of hostas in containers placed in a shady garden corner provides a great way to mix and match varieties.

Good Companions

Trees for hostas

Whatever the theme, size and aspect of your garden, the hostas within in it will do best if you can duplicate the woodland conditions they enjoy in the wild. Woodlands consist of shady areas as well as more open spaces among the tall-growing trees that provide the shade. Even with just two or three trees in your garden, there is a place where you can create a small woodland-style area suitable for growing hostas.

Suitable deciduous shade trees

When choosing trees, I greatly favor deciduous species, because they provide shade from spring to early winter, and provide you with an excellent mulch when they drop their leaves. During winter the sun also penetrates the bare branches and helps condition the soil, by keeping it from getting water-logged and perhaps souring. There is a large range of deciduous trees from which to choose; some are flowering species, a number of which are also perfumed.

The first shade trees I am going to recommend are Japanese maples, *Acer palmatum* (zones 6–8). Their spring and fall colors are bright and beautiful, yet they have a peaceful presence. Any or all of these really special trees would be very suitable for the shade garden, so I shall mention just a few favorites. For red leaves I recommend *Acer palmatum atropurpureum* 'O'kagami', 'Beni-otake', 'Bloodgood' and the stunning 'Beni-komachi'. In green, 'Osakazuki' is very famous, not so much for its spring green, but for its superb intense red fall color. I would also recommend 'Seiryu' because of its finely dissected green

OPPOSITE: The bold foliage of hostas works well with many other foliage and flowering plants.

RIGHT: The delicate reddish foliage of Japanese maples contrasts with the large green leaves of a hosta planting.

Japanese maples, here *Acer palmatum dissectum* 'Toyama Nishiki', always look great with hostas.

leaves. You might also like to have one or two maples with variegated leaves. These can be useful for lightening up dull places or for providing contrast to other trees with more somber colors. In this category I would suggest 'Shigitatsu-sawa', which is pale green with deep greenish brown veins that turn scarlet in fall, and 'Asahi-zuru' or 'Higasayama'. There is also the very beautiful two-toned 'Villa Taranto', which has green leaves overlaid with a delicate soft red. There are many more Japanese maples to choose from, so visit your local garden center or nursery to see what they have.

Betula species, the birches, look very much at home in woodland, and in my opinion they are some of the most beautiful, elegant and airy trees. Many of them have the added attraction of peeling bark. The only thing I can say against them is that they are greedy, so you must feed the plants growing near them.

There are about 60 species of birch, but I shall recommend just a few that I would hate to be without. For woodland my very first choice would be *Betula nigra* 'Heritage'(zones 4–9). This birch loves dampness, so it is commonly known as the river birch. It is fast growing and has glorious peeling bark in a lovely creamy pinkish orange color, which turns brown on the older trees. Next I would suggest *Betula albosinensis* (zones 5–8), which has wonderful peeling bark that is cream when first exposed and then turns coppery red with a hint of pink. This tree also grows rapidly and is rather large, so choose it only if you have the space. *Betula utilis* var. *jacquemontii* (zones 5–7) is an aristocrat with the most beautiful white bark, and recently Hillier's famous nursery in Wincester, England, developed a form of this treasure called 'Silver Shadow', which the nursery thinks is perhaps the most beautiful of all. It has startling white bark and drooping dark green leaves. There are many more birches of course, but these are my favorites. If you can manage a little group of birches, you will be rewarded by their beauty; their leaf canopy is light and delicate, the leaves soft green in spring, gold in the fall, and all are blessed with beautiful bark.

Nyssa species (tupelo) are deciduous trees noted particularly for their intense fall color. Fall color is important in the shade garden, because most of the underplanting – the hostas and all their companion plants – will be past their best, so deciduous trees that color beautifully have a real role to play. *Nyssa sylvatica* (zones 5–9), whose foliage turns scarlet, orange and yellow, is perhaps the most commonly grown. There is also *Nyssa sinensis* (zones 7–9), which is considered even more desirable. It has new growth that is red throughout the season and it produces a stunning display of red in the fall. The last *Nyssa* I shall mention is the cultivar 'Sheffield Park', which changes color earlier than the others mentioned and has brilliant orange-red hues. These trees, which revel in the dampness of a shade garden, are all highly recommended.

If you have both the space for a quite large tree and a suitable climate, I would suggest you consider *Davidia involucrata* (zones 6–8), commonly known as the dove tree or the handkerchief tree because its very large drooping white bracts look somewhat like handkerchiefs (but not at all like doves). Regardless, it is a very beautiful tree with a neat, upright shape and yellow fall coloring. Although eventually quite large, it is, in fact, a rather slow-growing tree. I should also mention that it takes a few years to flower, with the attendant white bracts, but even without flowers and bracts it is well worth growing.

There is also a truly gorgeous small tree called *Cercis canadensis* 'Forest Pansy', a variety of the eastern redbud (zones 5–9). It has large, heart-shaped leaves that are an astonishing deep red-purple and turn apri-

TOP: A maple provides some shade for this border of candelabra primulas (foreground) and hostas (background).

ABOVE: The rich red of *Cercis canadensis* 'Forest Pansy'.

cot, yellow and red in the fall. Another very beautiful North American tree is *Liquidamber styraciflua*, or sweetgum (zones 6–9). It is a superb pyramid-shaped tree with absolutely blazing fall color. It grows large, increasing in beauty with the years, and needs space to display its full beauty.

Two trees not yet mentioned are the deciduous conifer *Metasequoia glyptostroboides*, dawn redwood (zones 5–10), and *Taxodium distichum*, the swamp cypress (zones 5–10). These trees have feathery green leaves, shaggy green bark and stunning fall color of bronze and cinnamon. The swamp cypress likes to grow in water, but this is not necessary for its well being; just damp soil would be suitable for both. While they do grow tall, they are also quite slim and I cannot recommend them highly enough if you have room. These trees look just as good grown in groups as they do as single specimens.

Some flowering tree species

When considering flowering trees with perfumed blossoms, magnolias of almost any variety are superb (depending on species, hardiness varies but is generally zones 5–9 or 6–9). In my opinion paler rather than brighter colors look best because they make the shade garden look very peaceful and restful. Magnolias that impart a tranquil atmosphere are *Magnolia denudata* (white, elegant and perfumed), 'Athene' (white, flushed pink, scented), 'David Clulow' (pure white), 'Lotus' (creamy white), 'Manchu Fan' (white, purple stain at base, fragrant), 'Rouged Alabaster' (white, pink blush at base, very fragrant), 'Snow White' (erect small white flower, perfumed) and *M. x loebneri* 'Leonard Messel' (pale lavender-pink, scented). There are many more, of course, and the choice is yours, but those I have suggested are really stunning.

A splendid group of flowering trees are the dogwoods *Cornus florida* and *Cornus kousa* (zones 5–8). For shade gardens I do not think any *Cornus* could be better than the hybrid 'Eddie's White Wonder', which grows tall and pendulous and has lovely white flowers (really bracts, but to most gardeners the description "flowers" will do). In white, *Cornus florida* 'Cloud Nine' and 'Cherokee Princess' come to mind; then there are *florida* cultivars with variegated leaves such as 'Rainbow', 'Daybreak' and 'Sunset'. For pink flowers you could choose 'Spring Song' or 'Stokes Pink'. All these *Cornus florida* hybrids have, as well as beautiful "flowers", the most glorious fall colors. A little later in the season *Cornus kousa*, from Japan, blooms with similar bracts, though perhaps a little larger, and smaller leaves that turn red in fall. I would recommend 'China Girl' or 'Milky Way' in white, and the wonderful 'Satomi' in pink.

If your climate allows, include a *Prunus serrulata* (ornamental Japanese cherry) in your garden. It is one of the most beautiful of flowering trees. Not only are they a froth of blossom in the spring, but they very generously provide stunning tawny orange and yellow fall colors. Some Japanese cherries are

upright growers and are therefore not good at producing shade, but most have a spreading habit, which is excellent for hostas. I have never seen a Japanese cherry that wasn't beautiful, but I suggest that 'Mount Fuji' (white, fragrant), 'Pink Perfection' (pink, with bronze new leaves), 'Shirofugen' (white, faded pink, with copper-colored new growth), 'Taihaku', also known as Great White Cherry (pure white flowers, bronze-red young leaves), and 'Ukon' (pale yellowish, tinged green, pink flushed) would enhance any garden, shady or otherwise (all zones 6–8).

A superb cherry comes from Taiwan. This is *Prunus campanulata*, often called the Taiwan cherry or the bell-flowered cherry (zones 7–8). It has enormous numbers of cerise flowers early in the spring and is an absolute mecca for birds. If you plan to grow this splendid tree make sure it has plenty of space, since it grows large quite rapidly.

The wonderful fall color of *Cornus* 'Eddie's White Wonder'. Dogwoods are excellent companions to hostas, providing spring color with their flowers and late-season color as the leaves turn to orange and red.

Kalmias make great hosta companions.

TOP: Kalmia 'Sarah' with 'Blue Angel' in the foreground.

ABOVE: The delicate *Kalmia* 'Pink Charm' with the striking leaves of 'June'.

OPPOSITE: A large bank covered in hostas and their favorite companion plants.

Shrubs for hostas

There are shrubs that like dappled shade and, in turn, provide shade to other plants. Discretion needs to be exercised here because you don't want to fill up all the available space and then have no room for desirable shade garden perennials, such as hostas. However, I suggest that strategically placed rhododendrons and kalmias add greatly to the structure of the garden and to its beauty. These are both shrubs for temperate climates, with certain species and varieties surviving at zone 5, but most at zones 6 and 7 or above.

If your climate and soil are suitable (rhododendrons like a slightly acidic soil), there is a large selection of rhododendrons from which to choose, but I particularly like scented rhododendrons. Many of these are species in pale colors that look good in a woodland-style hosta garden.

The lovely shrub *Kalmia latifolia* (zones 5–9), the mountain laurel or calico bush, was sadly neglected for many years until 1961, when Richard Janes of the Connecticut Agricultural Station started a breeding program. The *Kalmia* is a low- to medium-sized shrub with leathery, evergreen leaves. In late spring the plant is smothered in small, saucer-shaped flowers in lovely colors of pink, red and white, bi-colored or banded. It likes the same conditions as rhododendrons: a moist, acidic soil and light shade.

ABOVE: *Anemone x hybrida*, or Japanese anemone, can be invasive but its fall flowers make it a very worthwhile addition to the garden.

All *Kalmia* are very desirable, from the species *K. latifolia* in soft pink to the brighter, more spectacular modern hybrids. It should be mentioned that the buds of the *Kalmia* are so beautiful that you wouldn't think the flowers could be even better – but they are. My favorites are 'Sarah' (an astonishing red), 'Pink Charm' (deep pink buds that open lighter), 'Nipmuck' (scarlet buds that open to soft pink flowers), 'Madeline' (the world's first double pink and white), 'Elf' (a dwarf with large white flowers opening from pink buds) and 'Stillwood' (pure white). In the banded range, I like 'Bullseye'. Even two or three of these lovely shrubs in your woodland garden would enhance it greatly.

Another shrub, also native to North America, is *Fothergilla*. There are two species, *F. major* (zones 5–8), large fothergilla, and *F. gardenii* (zones 5–9), dwarf fothergilla. Both like cool, moist, acidic soils. In spring the bush has white fluffy, upright flowers that are scented, but its real glory is in the fall, when large blue-green leaves turn the most dazzling colors of red, purple, orange and yellow. These do not grow very tall – perhaps from 3 to 6 ft. (1 to 2 m). *F. gardenii* grows only about 3 ft. (1 m) high and has blue leaves and astonishing fall colors.

ABOVE LEFT: The unusual *Arisaema candidissimum*.
ABOVE RIGHT: Aquilegias are particularly beautiful planted among hostas.

Companion shade plants for hostas

There are so many gorgeous shade garden plants that work beautifully with hostas that it is difficult to know where to start, so I think it would be a good idea to do it alphabetically!

My first subject is therefore *Ajuga*, bugleweed, a very useful ground cover that looks good among other woodland plants. The most often used is *A. reptans* (zones 3–9) with its dark green leaves and azure-blue flowers. 'Jungle Beauty' is a taller-growing variety at 12 in. (30 cm) and a purple-leafed form called 'Atropurpurea' is also very attractive. Both spread with enthusiasm.

The delightfully modest little wood anemone, *Anemone nemorosa* (zones 4–8), pops up in early spring before plants like hostas have got out of bed. It has simple, single flowers that are white, pale pink or light blue. The wood anemones spread quietly and, just when other more assertive plants are making their spring statements, they unobtrusively disappear, only to make a welcome re-appearance 12 months later.

Another, very different anemone is the Japanese anemone, *A.* x *hybrida* (zones 4–8). There is nothing modest about this plant – it is very invasive – but because it flowers in the fall it is valuable. It is also lovely and has tall stems of single flowers in pale or deeper pink. The most admired of these anemones is the white form *A.* x *hybrida* 'Honorine Jobert'. They all have territorial ambitions and must be kept firmly in check; each year I cull most of them, but I still have enough for a nice fall show.

Aquilegia species, charmingly known as columbines, are the darlings of most gardens, whether in sun or shade. They are particularly beautiful when planted among hostas. Their bell-shaped, spurred flowers add a delicate note to the sturdy hosta leaves beneath. The best species for shade is *A. vulgaris* (zones 3–8), granny's bonnet, which comes in lots of colors, including white, pink, blue, yellow and purple, many with contrasting cups or centers. They are not long-lived perennials, but this is not a worry for gardeners, as they seed very freely.

Arisaema are curious plants with hooded flowers enclosing a thin spadix (something that looks like a pencil). The dark ones, like *A. sikokianum* (zones 5–9), look like wicked arum lilies, whereas *A. candidissimum* (zones 6–9) is a pink-and-white striped beauty with stunning large oval leaves. *A. concinnum* (zones 6–10) is tall and stately with a whorl of narrow leaves at the top of the stalk. The flowers on this one tend to be hidden underneath the leaves. In green stripes you can have *A. triphyllum* (zones 4–9) or *A. jacquemontii* (zones 7–9), both of which are attractive. In the same green colors are the flowers of *A. ringens* (zones 5–9), but they also have dramatic brown edges. Perfect for a little nook is the mouse plant, *A. praecox* (zones 6–9), whose "mice" hide underneath the leaves. *Pinellia* (zones 6–9) are of the same family as *Arisaema* and to

A wonderful planting of trees, shrubs and flowers with a striking variegated hosta as the eye-catching focal point.

me look much the same. They also are a pleasant green with the same hood-like spathes, but can be very invasive.

Aruncus dioicus (zones 3–7), commonly known as goatsbeard, resembles a big white-flowered astilbe. It has lovely ferny green foliage and very large plumes of flowers. It is quite imposing and looks just right blooming over an underplanting of hostas.

Astilbe species love damp conditions and partial shade. They kindly flower in the summer when others are finished and rely on their leaves for interest. Astilbes have delicate-looking ferny leaves and plumes of flowers. I particularly like, and would recommend, *Astilbe* 'Fanal', an Arendsii hybrid which has the most gorgeous crimson flowers, 'Weisse Gloria', with white flowers, and 'Bressingham Beauty' and the graceful 'Betsy Cuperus', both of which are pink. 'Granat' is another one to try; it has bright red flowers. (All Arendsii hybrids are zones 6–10.) Both before and after they flower, astilbes' leaves look lovely, soft and refined.

Brunnera macrophylla, Siberian bugloss (zones 3–7), has a flower like a forget-me-not, but is vastly superior. It has beautiful oval, pointed leaves that should guarantee this plant a place in the shade garden, even if it didn't flower. It has dainty, intensely blue flowers on long, thin stems. *Brunnera macrophylla* 'Dawson's White' (syn. 'Variegata') has very wide white margins. I have found it difficult to grow well, but it is worth a little extra effort.

Cardiocrinum giganteum is commonly called the giant Himalayan lily (zones 7–9), but that is the only common thing about it. It has a splendid flower, cream with reddish rays, and the most pervasive sweet scent. If this were not enough to make it a treasure, it also has beautiful large soft green leaves. Then, to add the finishing touch, the flower stems are about 6 ft. (2 m) high. When the large seed pods appear, they stand tall and commanding for many months, like soldiers on parade. Eventually they release an astonishing number of seeds and, where the habitat is ideal (i.e., damp and shaded, with humus-rich soil), they will soon turn into a lily forest. Each plant takes some years to flower, but where they are seeding freely there are always more coming on.

Cimicifuga racemosa, black cohosh (zones 3–8), is very pretty in a group as a companion planting for hostas. It has tall, bottle-brush-like flowers above and ferny leaves below. It is not perhaps a perennial that you couldn't live without, but I think it has its place and again, it is easy to grow.

I have always grown the ferny-leafed *Corydalis ochroleuca* (zones 6–8), a delicate-looking plant that has pretty little creamy white flowers, tipped green. *Corydalis lutea* (zones 5–8) is similar, but with a yellow flower. In

TOP: *Astilbe* Arendsii hybrid 'Fanal'

MIDDLE: *Brunnera macrophylla* 'Dawson's White' has superb big leaves and dainty violet flowers.

ABOVE: *Cardiocrinum giganteum*, or Himalayan lily, is suitable only for temperate zones (7–9). If you are able to grow it, it makes quite an impact in the shade garden.

TOP: *Epimedium sulphureum* is an excellent, trouble-free woodland plant.

ABOVE: Some unusual flowers for the shade garden: *Trillium chloropetalum* 'Alba' (left), *Fritillaria cirrhosa* (center), *Erythronium* 'Pagoda' (center below) and *Fritillaria meleagris* (right).

suitable climates, both are quick to spread. *Corydalis flexuosa* (zones 6–8) will fill you with delight in the spring. What a color! The flowers are the most intense blue. There are various forms available, including 'Blue Panda', 'China Blue' and 'Père David'. There is also a form with bronze-purple leaves, but the same rich blue flowers. As with the other *Corydalis*, they spread delightfully.

Dicentra formosa, Western bleeding heart (zones 4–8), from North America could probably be called a delightful weed, but I must emphasize the delightful rather than the weed, because this plant is so pretty. It has delicate, fern-like leaves and little bell-shaped flowers, in pink or pure white. There are various cultivars such as 'Bountiful' (deep pink), 'Stuart Boothman' (pink), 'Langtrees' (silver-gray leaves, cream and pink flowers) and 'Zestful' (pale pink flowers). *Dicentra* spreads like crazy, but the plants are easy to pull out. I just let them go because they are so light and airy they do not smother anything, and certainly not hostas! *Dicentra spectabilis* (zones 3–9) is commonly known as bleeding heart. I have found it to be entirely different from *D. formosa* because in my garden it seems to disappear after a year or two, but in other places is long-lived. Whatever your circumstances, it is worth the effort because it has charming pink-and-white, or pure white, flowers that look like a lady's locket.

Digitalis purpurea and hybrids (zones 4–8), or foxgloves, are happy in sun or shade and come in various hues of purple, white or salmon. I always think that white foxgloves are the best but, of course, that is a matter of choice. They stand tall above most hostas and create a stunning background. They seed prolifically, but if you have surplus plants, your friends will probably be thrilled to accept them.

Disporum species (zones 4–9), or fairy bells, is another pretty plant that spreads. It has bell-shaped creamy yellow flowers and the form I have in my garden has variegated leaves. It "walks around" a bit, but looks well among hostas and other woodland plants. Of course if you wish you can dispose of what you do not want, but it is not a bulky plant, so you might want to do as I do and let it wander at will.

Epimedium species (zones 5–9) are very good woodland plants whose interesting leaves contrast nicely with hostas. The leaves are more or less heart-shaped, red in some species and green in others, often turning bronze in winter. Its little flowers are yellow through to reddish tones, and are often nearly obscured by the leaves. The trick is to cut the old leaves down in late winter, allowing the dainty flowers to be seen. It's a very nice, trouble-free plant to own.

Fritillaria are beautiful aristocrats that need a special place in the hosta garden where they will not be smothered. While the hostas are still getting their act together, these beautiful little bulbs are flowering. They have nodding bells in the most unusual colors, including green, brown, purple and white. Sometimes the bells are banded, sometimes spotted and sometimes checkered. Before I reach my dotage I would like to have amassed a huge collection of fritillaries. Currently I have *F. meleagris*, the commonest, but no less beautiful for that (zones 3–8), *F. uva-vulpis* (syn. *F. assyriaca* of gardens, zones 7–9), *F. graeca* (zones 6–9), *F. alfredae* (zones 6–8), *F. crassifolia* (zones 6–8), *F. lusitanica* (zones 7–9), *F. cirrhosa* (zones 6–8), *F. messanensis* (zones 8–10) and *F. acmopetala* (zones 6–8). They are all quite special.

Gunnera manicata (zones 7–10) is huge, up to 8 ft. (2.5 m) high, and looks like an enormous rhubarb. Somehow it seems incongruous to call it a perennial, but it is. It has two uses in the woodland hosta garden. One is as a splendid architectural background, the other as a shade producer. When the rather prickly, coarse leaves die down in late fall it is necessary to remove them or else they will smother everything underneath.

Helleborus orientalis (zones 4–9) make splendid companion plants for hostas, not least because they flower in winter or very early spring, providing beauty while hostas are still only thinking about poking their noses up to test the air. Hybrids of Oriental hellebores have absolutely charming, saucer-shaped flowers in subtle, soft colors, from white through to ruby pink, and maroon, purple and reddish shades. The flowers have a boss of stamens resembling a crown. The leaves of hellebores are rather coarse, so it is a good idea to chop them right back before flowering time, then feed the plant well and you will be able to see the divine flowers clearly. They seed and hybridize prolifically, so you never know what new color you might find.

Heuchera species (coral bells, zones 4–8) are easy to grow in either sun or filtered shade. Their scalloped leaves are often marbled and veined, and

Helleborus orientalis flower early in the season, before the hostas, and the colors are subtle and soft.

TOP AND ABOVE: *Hyacinthoides*, or bluebells, make wonderful companion plants for hostas. They create a dazzling display for little effort, but can become invasive.

some come in the most amazing blend of colors, from green with white to bronze, purple, burgundy and red. These striking leaves contrast very nicely with hostas, and as an added bonus they have flowers, which are borne on naked stems, in white, pink or red. You really need a good-sized clump for the little flowers to make an impact, but in the end I think it is the leaves that really steal the show.

Hyacinthoides (syn. *Endymion*), or bluebells, are wonderful companion plants for hostas and other shade-lovers. The most commonly seen are the Spanish bluebell, *H. hispanicus* (zones 4–9), and the smaller English bluebell, *H. non-scripta* (zones 4–9). The thing about bluebells is that they flower early and prolifically and create a dazzling display without any care and attention at all. While they are flowering only the earliest hostas are in leaf, and by the time the hostas are looking their best in fresh spring growth, the bluebells have faded. While bluebells are invasive, they can also be considered a weed-suppressing ground cover. As well as the traditional blue bluebell, there are pink, mauve and white versions of this pretty bulb, but to my mind, although attractive, they do not have the impact of the wonderful blue.

Kirengeshoma palmata (zones 5–8) is not very well-known, and perhaps you would not be filled with despair if you did not own it, but its long, wide green leaves with pointed ends and pretty yellow drooping flowers, which come in late summer, form a nice contrast with hostas.

Ligularias make absolutely splendid companion plants, particularly for hostas, as their handsome leaves are a good foil to those of the hostas. They are large and some are purple, some green. *Ligularia dentata* 'Desdemona' (zones 4–8) is my favorite because of its big shiny, kidney-shaped purple leaves. It has orange-yellow daisy-like flowers that I am not so keen on, but which many people admire. A different species, *L. stenocephala* (zones 4–8), has a cultivar called 'The Rocket', because of its long, slender yellow flowers. A large, green-leafed version with yellow spots all over is called *L. tussilanginea* 'Aureomaculata' (syn. *Farfugium japonicum* 'Aureomaculatum', zones 7–10). It is, I think, perhaps more novel than beautiful, but I still like to have it in my garden. It is commonly known as 'The Leopard', which is quite apt.

Meconopsis, the blue Himalayan poppy, really is to die for. Planted among smaller-growing blue hostas like 'Dorset Blue', it is a wonderful sight. The most well-known species is *M. betonicifolia* (zones 7–8), with its heavenly pure sky-blue flowers. Unfortunately, like many aristocrats, it is very particular indeed. Although these poppies like the same conditions as hostas – damp, humus-rich soil that never dries out – that does not necessarily mean that they will thrive. In my experience, it is only through trial and error that you finally find the right place for them. Even if you do find such a place, Himalayan poppies are very often monocarpic, which means they flower only once, and they are at best a short-lived perennial. If you wish to have plants coming on all the time, they are quite easy to grow from fresh seed. All this might sound like too much trouble, but these glorious flowers are worth it. *Meconopsis grandis* (zones 5–8) is superbly dark blue, but perhaps the most beautiful of all are the hybrids crossed between *M. betonicifolia* and *M. grandis* called *Meconopsis* x *sheldonii*. The most stunning of these forms is called 'Slieve Donard'. People seeing *Meconopsis* for the first time are often startled by their glorious blues.

Then there are other colored *Meconopsis* that don't have the astonishing blue of the above species, but are still well worth having. *M. cambrica* (zones 6–8) is the Welsh poppy, and comes in pretty yellow or orange. It seeds freely. *M. regia* (zones 8–9) has silky, hairy leaves and in summer large yellow flowers. Even in winter its leaves look attractive. *M. napaulensis* (zones 8–9), the satin poppy, can have flowers of blue, pink or red. Mine are red, and very attractive too, but really nothing matches the heavenly blues.

Omphalodes cappadocica (zones 6–8) is another blue flower. This time the little flowers are of the forget-me-not variety, which look good in a woodland setting among hostas. The leaves are deep green and evergreen, though hard frosts are not acceptable and could kill the plant. It spreads gently, if happy.

TOP: The handsome leaves *of Ligularia stenocephala* provide a nice complement to the leaves of the hosta.

ABOVE: If you can grow any of the *Meconopsis* species (zones 7–9) they are well worth while. As a change from the vivid blues of the Himalayan poppy, this *M. napaulensis* has satiny red blooms.

ABOVE: *Primula pulverulenta* is a vigorous plant with deep pinky red flowers.

BELOW: A mass of candelabra primulas in yellows and pinks with hostas in front. The large plant center left is a *Cardiocrinum giganteum*, Himalayan lily, and to the bottom right is *Polygonatum* x *hybridum*.

Polygonatum x *hybridum* (common Solomon's seal, zones 6–9) is one of my very favorite plants to associate with hostas in the shade garden. It has arching stems of light green leaves, and from the axils of the leaves hang little white, green-tipped tubular bells. Bold clumps look best and are not difficult to grow because common Solomon's seal is a real spreader, delightfully so, in my opinion, though some people consider it first cousin to a weed.

Primula species, particularly the candelabra type, are absolutely glorious when planted with hostas. Candelabra primulas are tall, the flowers rising in tiers above the hostas in the most luscious colors, and they bloom for a long time. Of course they like damp, semi-shaded conditions and, if provided with these essentials, are easy to grow and have seedlings appearing all the time. *Primula japonica* (Japanese primrose, zones 3–8) is probably the best-known of the species. It is deciduous, vigorous and usually red, but two forms of it are particularly desirable: 'Miller's Crimson', which has very red buds and lighter red flowers, and 'Postford White', which has an orange eye. Unfortunately this one is not long lived, but it does reproduce itself exactly from seed, as does 'Miller's Crimson'.

Primula pulverulenta (zones 4–8) is a great favorite with those who grow primulas. It is tall and vigorous, with large, lettuce-like leaves and flower stems covered with farina (a sort of mealy bloom). The flowers are a deep pinky red with purple eyes. It would be really difficult to choose one candelabra primula above another, but *P. pulverulenta* is certainly a candidate for a garden "Oscar."

Orange is not a color I particularly like, so I am going to call the beautiful *P. bulleyana* (zones 5–8) strong apricot. It is really lovely and, with *P. cockburniana* (zones 5–8), which is monocarpic so you have to grow the next lot from seed, makes a nice contrast with other plants. Although some purists keep species and colors separate I think they look wonderful mixed up together. Their grace enhances the hostas and many other shade-loving plants. *Primula burmanica* (zones 5–8) has reddish purple flowers and is particularly vigorous. All of the above species hybridize freely, producing a wonderful mix of colors. The 'Harlow Carr' hybrids are a very famous and complex group produced by such hybridization.

Hostas and candelabra primulas work very well together, with the flowers rising in tiers above the hostas.

TOP: *Primula helodoxa*
ABOVE: The low-growing *Pulmonaria* 'David Ward', with its hairy, silver-edged leaves.

Primula helodoxa (zones 5–8) is an evergreen, and its vivid yellow flowers have the most delightful perfume. If it is suited to the site, it seeds very freely, so much so that some people like to confine it to a separate place. *P. helodoxa* provides a lovely bright splash amongst the darker candelabra primulas and looks stunning among hostas, particularly those with gold or yellow in their leaves.

There are a great many species of primula – all beautiful – but many are not really suitable for growing among sturdy hostas. There is one summer-flowering species (whereas the candelabra primulas are spring flowers) called *P. florindae* (giant cowslip, zones 3–8), which is tall and sturdy with pendant, bell-shaped yellow flowers, or, more rarely, they are a reddish apricot color. It grows well with hostas and also lengthens the primula flowering period.

Pulmonaria species (zones 5–8) are so much nicer than their name, which somehow sounds like a lung disease; in fact, its common name is lungwort. They are low-growing plants with hairy leaves. Some leaves are plain green but many are beautifully spotted with silver or splashed with white. The flowers are blue, pink, red or white and last for a long time. They look good in front of hostas because their leaves create a very pleasant contrast.

Rodgersia are splendid foliage plants that also produce flowers. *Rodgersia aesculifolia* (zones 5–8) has large, bronzy green leaves that are nicely crinkled, and white flowers. *Rodgersia pinnata* 'Superba' (zones 5–8) has handsome green-flushed bronze leaves and bright pink flowers reminiscent of an astilbe.

Sanguinaria canadensis (bloodroot, zones 3–9) offers a real challenge. The challenge is not in growing the plant, as that is not difficult, but rather in seeing its enchanting white flowers before, with unseemly haste, the petals fall off. The flower stems appear before the leaves, and each is topped with a bulb-shaped bud that opens to a single flower. The leaves come up folded and vertical before they unfold quite large and lobed. It is a fascinating plant and should be used in a special spot. There is a double form called *S. c.* 'Flore Pleno' that does not have the attractive simplicity of the single version. It is commonly called bloodroot because, if you cut the fleshy roots, they bleed a red juice.

Symphytum species (comfrey, zones 5–9) can be described as a ground cover or an invasive weed. Used carefully, they can be very useful to cover awkward places in the garden. The coarse leaves are quite acceptable and the creamy bell-shaped flowers are very pretty. Keep in mind that these plants are only for rough places, because they will smother anything in their way.

The white splashed on the leaves of *Pulmonaria* 'Beth's Blue' can work very well at the front of a hosta planting.

Tiarella species, or foamflowers, are very useful early-blooming little plants that associate well with hostas. Their heart-shaped leaves are very pleasant and, when topped with abundant clusters of either pink or white flowers, these plants are a fetching sight. *T. cordifolia* (zones 3–7) and *T. wherryi* (zones 5–9) are the most commonly grown.

Tricyrtis hirta (zones 4–9), known by the particularly unattractive name of toad lily, is a strange and interesting plant that is nothing like a lily. It is not overtly showy, though when it flowers in fall there is not too much competition around. The arching stems are quite tall, about 3 ft. (1 m), and carry flowers between the leaf axils. Its flowers are bell-shaped and white with heavy purple-lilac spotting so the overall effect is light purple. They spread easily but are never a problem because the stems are quite skinny and rise high above the plants beneath. It is an easy, unfussy and unique plant.

Uvularia species (merrybells, zones 3–8) are not used as much as they deserve to be, for they are unusual and pretty plants. Long, bell-shaped flowers of a bright yellow hang down gracefully from the slim green stems. They flower generously for quite a long time over spring and summer.

CLEMATIS

I feel clematis are so special they deserve highlighting in this chapter. Clematis are seldom mentioned or considered as companions for other plants, apart from roses. This seems strange because they have so much to offer a garden. Also, they themselves need other plants to either ramble among or climb up and most gardens, whether they feature hostas or not, have a tree or two, and plantings of shrubs and perennials, and this is just what clematis need.

Clematis can add an extra dimension to your garden, especially if it contains some hosta-shading trees. If you have not previously grown clematis, start with the easy and exuberant species *Clematis montana* (zones 6–9). It will romp away up a host tree and, when grown to its full potential, is a wonderful sight. A note of caution must be sounded here: the tree needs to be large and sturdy because in the right climate *C. montana* grows quite rampantly. Of course you could always prune the clematis, but I think the true beauty of this climber is in its amazing waterfalls of bloom in the spring.

There are quite a few cultivars of *C. montana*, but I greatly favor *C. montana alba* (syn. 'Snowflake') which fits nicely into a woodland scene. If you prefer a climber that is pink, the ever popular *C. montana rubens* is for you.

You do not have to grow a huge climber, because there are many very beautiful, large-flowered clematis that grow to only 3–6 ft. (1–2 m) and can be pruned back to grow

again the following year. These plants are very useful and decorative when climbing up smaller trees or shrubs. They make a pretty background for the hostas beneath.

There is a wide choice of clematis available and, if you choose mid-season flowering types, you can extend the flowering season of your clematis. Should you wish to have a white theme, I have found 'Henryi' and 'Marie Boisselot' very satisfactory. But there are lots of beautifully colored varieties also, including 'Dr. Ruppel' (deep rose pink), 'Mrs. N. Thompson' (bluish purple with a dark pink central band), good old 'Nelly Moser' (pale mauve, white-centered band, the whole flower fading with age); and 'Niobe' (very dark red). The good thing about these particular clematis is that you cut them right back in the winter so you do not have untidy vines clinging to the host. All is left neat and tidy, awaiting the early summer.

For late summer flowering, and particularly for clematis to ramble through shrubs, you could consider 'Allanah' (red with dark stamens), 'Hagley Hybrid' (rosy mauve), 'Rouge Cardinal' (velvety crimson), 'Comtesse de Bouchaud' (bright mauve-pink), and 'Lady Betty Balfour' (gorgeous azure blue). All the above varieties are hardy to zone 4.

I recently started to consider growing clematis as a ground cover, for want of a better word. What I really mean is twining it through perennials at ground level. In the context of a hosta garden I do not suggest you use a whole mass, but simply a plant here and there to add interest. I think that small flowers would be the most appropriate. For this purpose, I would choose *C. viticella*

(zones 5–9) and *C. texensis* (zones 4–9) varieties. *C. viticella* hybrids have small flowers that appear over a period of three months, and *C. texensis* varieties have pitcher-shaped flowers that are often red. They are also relatively long flowering. My favorite *C. viticella* is called 'Madame Julia Correvon', and is a bright, clean, rosy red. Then there is the very free-flowering 'Etoile de Violette' in deep purple, and 'Abundance' in bright mauve pink. In *C. texensis* cultivars 'Sir Trevor Lawrence' is absolutely gorgeous in luminous crimson, 'Gravetye Beauty' is rich ruby red and 'Princess of Wales' is a deep, vibrant pink.

Clematis need a cool root run that never dries out. They also like plenty of humus and need to be planted deeper in the ground than they were in the pot they came in. (This is not the normal practice when transferring potted plants into the soil.) They have only one drawback, but it is major: they can suffer from clematis wilt, which causes the plant to collapse. If this happens, cut the clematis right back, spray it with Benlate (benomyl) or something similar and in time it will likely recover. If, when you plant the clematis, you use a live fungicide, i.e., one that incorporates *Trichoderma* spp., there should be no problem. The *viticella* and *texensis* hybrids are fortunately not affected by wilt; nor for that matter have I ever seen a *C. montana* with this problem.

So, when you are thinking about companion planting among your hostas, give more than passing consideration to the beautiful clematis, because they have much to offer.

A variety of *Clematis* among hosta plantings.

Catalog of Hostas

The list below gives details of the hostas mentioned in this book, plus many more. The name and date beside some of the hostas refer to the breeder and year the hosta was registered. If there is no date or name, these details are unknown. All hostas appear in the spring, with flowers emerging over the summer season. The exact timing of this depends on the hosta and local climate. However, hostas are primarily grown for their foliage; the flowers, when they appear, are an added bonus. The measurements given for height and width are approximations only, and the metric conversions have been rounded to the nearest 5 cm.

OPPOSITE: A planting of hostas, clematis and candelabra primulas.

RIGHT: A planting of hostas, *H. undulata, H. 'Decorata'* and *H. lancifolia,* with candelabra primulas.

Abba Dabba Do (Advent)
This hosta is one of the newer gold-margined varieties. It has large green wavy leaves with gold margins, and the flowers are lavender. It grows to 24 in. high and 36 in. wide (60 cm by 90 cm).

Abiqua Drinking Gourd (Walden-West 1988)
A beautiful, heavily puckered blue hosta that really does makes you think you could drink out of its puckered leaves. It grows about 20 in. high and 45 in. wide (50 cm by 110 cm), and is highly recommended. It has white flowers and an open, mounding habit.

Ace of Hearts (Barrett)
A well-named hosta with blue-green leaves and a neat, rounded habit of growth. It grows approximately 20 in. high and 24 in. wide (50 cm by 60 cm). It produces a profusion of pale lavender flowers. The leaves have a very heavy texture and retain their metallic blue color all season.

'Aristocrat'   'Big Daddy'

Allan P. McConnell (McConnell-Seaver 1980)
This little white-margined green hosta has stood
the test of time and is widely planted as an edging
plant. It is 8 in. high and 18 in. wide (20 cm by 45
cm) and looks very good in a pot or mixed with
other small hostas.

Anne Arett (Arett)
Ruffled, lance-shaped leaves in chartreuse with a
white edge make this little 10 in. high and 8 in.
wide (25 cm by 20 cm) hosta a very useful edger.

Antioch (Tompkins-Ruh 1979)
A splendid plant that has, deservedly, won many
American awards. It has mottled green leaves with
cream margins that later turn white. It grows to about
2 ft. high and 3 ft. wide (60 cm by 90 cm). I like the
way the leaves bend over, making a nice mound. It
has lavender flowers and is very similar to the highly
regarded British hosta called 'Spinners'.

Aristocrat (Walters Gardens)
A new and very attractive hosta. It is well bred
and is a sport of the famous 'Hadspen Blue'. It has
smooth light blue leaves with elegant cream
margins and lavender flowers. It measures 8 in.
high and 14 in. wide (20 cm by 35 cm).

Aspen Gold (Grapes 1970)
This is a very good gold that does not lose its
color in the summer. It grows to about 20 in. high
and 36 in. wide (50 cm by 90 cm) and has heavy,
beautifully cupped leaves and white flowers.
Although rather slow growing, it is an
outstanding plant.

August Moon (Langfeldex-Summer 1968)
A lovely hosta with rugose and greenish yellow
leaves in spring, but flat and yellow leaves by
summer. Growing 20 in. high and 30 in. wide
(50 cm by 75 cm), it appreciates some shade,
as do most yellows. 'August Moon' has been used
extensively in breeding, and also mutates into
some variegated forms, including the gorgeous
'September Sun'. It has white flowers.

Aurora Borealis (Wayside 1986)
This beautiful plant is quite similar to 'Frances
Williams'. It has very rugose blue-green leaves
with yellow margins. It grows to about 24 in. high
and 45 in. wide (60 cm by 110 cm). It is superb,
despite its susceptibility to necrosis (melt-out).

'Blue Blazes'

Big Daddy (Aden 1976)
This is such a good name for this award-winning big blue hosta, which grows 2 ft. high and 3 ft. wide (60 cm by 90 cm). It has white flowers and its deep blue leaves are heart-shaped and very puckered. Some claim it is pest resistant.

Big Mama (Aden 1976)
This is an *H. sieboldiana* selection and its leaves are bluer than those of 'Big Daddy'. It's bigger too at 3 ft. by 3 ft. (90 cm by 90 cm). A wonderful background plant with attractive white flowers.

Birchwood Blue (Shaw 1986)
The wonderful crinkled blue leaves make this hosta very attractive. What is also attractive is that it holds its glorious color all season. It has white flowers and is 16 in. high and 30 in. wide (40 cm by 75 cm).

Birchwood Parky's Gold (Shaw 1986)
I really like this vigorous gold hosta. It has heart-shaped leaves that become a rich yellow color with age. It is a very neat and pleasing plant, and provides a nice contrast among a blue or green group of hostas. In midsummer pale lavender-blue flowers appear. It is 16 in. high and 30 in. wide (40 cm by 75 cm).

Blond Elf
This pretty hosta grows into a neat mound 8 in. high and 24 in. wide (20 cm by 60 cm). Its lance-shaped leaves are pale gold and it has lavender flowers.

Blue Angel (Aden 1986)
Now this is what everyone thinks a blue hosta should be. It's large, 3 ft. high and 4 ft. wide (90 cm by 120 cm), and has huge, very blue leaves that are heavily textured. Its flowers are white. A wonderfully good background plant.

Blue Arrow (Anderson 1992)
This well-named hosta has blue leaves that point upwards. It grows to about 10 in. high and 18 in. wide (25 cm by 45 cm) with white flowers. It looks particularly pretty in a pot.

Blue Blazes (Vaughn 1988)
This extremely blue hosta has cupped leaves and lavender flowers. It is rather large at 30 in. high and 35 in. wide (75 cm by 90 cm).

Blue Cadet (Aden 1974)

It is very important to have plants which are suitable for the front of a border, and 'Blue Cadet' is a particularly good candidate. It has good substance and color, and received the Nancy Minks Award from the American Hosta Society in 1986. It grows to approximately 16 in. high and 28 in. wide (40 cm by 70 cm).

Blue Cups

This blue hosta, despite its size, 16 in. high by 28 in. wide (40 cm by 70 cm), has a very neat compact habit of growth, graced by lavender flowers.

Blue Ice (Benedict 1987)

This hosta has intensely blue heart-shaped leaves that are cupped and of heavy substance. It grows 8 in. high and 8 in. wide (20 cm by 20 cm), and has pale lavender flowers.

Blue Mammoth (Aden)

This powder-blue hosta is enormous at 2 ft. high and 3 ft. wide (60 cm by 90 cm), making a stunning specimen or great background. Its leaves are heavily corrugated and its flowers are white. If you like plants that make a statement, this is for you.

Blue Moon

This small, slow-growing, clump-forming plant has broad, heart-shaped leaves that are a rich blue-green colour. Its leaves are about 3 in. (8 cm) long and in summer it bears white flowers. It is useful at the front of a border and also as a ground cover. It is 5 in. high and 8 in. wide (12 cm by 20 cm).

Blue Seer (Aden)

This is a form of *H. sieboldiana* that is heavily puckered and an intense blue color. Not very different from the species, it likes some shade and its white flowers appear in summer. It is 2 ft. high and 4 ft. wide (60 cm by 120 cm).

Blue Skies (Smith 1998)

At 9 in. high and 12 in. wide (25 cm by 30 cm) this hosta is short and is very useful as a front border plant. Its leaves are steely blue-green and it has lavender-white flowers. It is from the famous Tardiana group of hostas, which are all lovely.

Blue Umbrellas (Aden 1976)

This strong blue hosta is excellent placed at the back of a border. It won the American Hosta Society's Blue Award in 1987. It grows 3 ft. high and 4 ft. wide (90 cm by 120 cm) and has white flowers.

Blue Wedgwood (Smith 1988)

This is another blue Tardiana and is named after the famous blue pottery made by Wedgwood & Sons. All hostas in this family are very beautiful. In midsummer, pale lavender flowers appear. It's 14 in. high and 24 in. wide (35 cm by 60 cm).

Bressingham Blue (Bloom)

This very pleasant blue hosta has white flowers and grows about 20 in. high and 24 in. wide (50 cm by 60 cm).

Bright Glow (Aden)

This is a rare, and very useful, small gold hosta, which is said to be pest resistant. It grows 12 in. high and 16 in. wide (30 cm by 40 cm) and has heavily textured gold leaves.

Bright Lights (Aden-Klehm)

This lovely plant is a personal favorite. It is soft and pretty and has puckered gold leaves with a streaked blue margin and white flowers. It grows 14 in. high and 24 in. wide (35 cm by 60 cm).

Brim Cup (Aden 1986)

Leaves of this hosta are rich green and cupped, with a wide creamy white margin. It has lavender flowers and grows quickly to 12 in. in height and 16 in. in width (30 cm by 40 cm).

Buckshaw Blue (Smith 1986)

This is a hosta with a wealth of awards, including the Midwest A.H.S. Blue Award (1980), the Nancy Minks Award (1976) and an Award of Merit from the Wisley Trials. It resembles the splendid *H.* 'Tokudama' but has deeper blue heart-shaped and cupped leaves. It has white flowers in early summer and grows 12 in. high and 24 in. wide (30 cm by 60 cm).

Camelot (Smith 1988)

Yet another from the Tardiana group. This very good blue-green hosta is not readily available. It reaches 15 in. in height and 22 in. in width (40 cm by 55 cm) and has lavender flowers.

Candy Hearts

This hosta is not well-known but has lovely cupped, heart-shaped leaves in a rather unusual gray-green color. It grows about 16 in. high and 28 in. wide (40 cm by 70 cm) and has lavender flowers.

Carol (Williams 1986)

A very pretty hosta with white margins that set off dark green, oval and glaucous leaves. It is 20 in. high and 36 in. wide (50 cm by 90 cm) and has lavender flowers.

'Chinese Sunrise'

Celebration (Aden 1978)

A small but very bright hosta that is 10 in. high and 14 in. wide (25 cm by 35 cm). Its lance-shaped leaves are cream, turning white, with a green margin. It also has lavender flowers.

Chinese Sunrise (Summers)

This attractive plant has thin, lance-shaped yellow leaves with a narrow green margin. Later in the season, the yellow turns chartreuse green. The plant makes a nice mound for a border and lavender flowers emerge in late summer. It is 14 in. high and 28 in. wide (35 cm by 70 cm).

Color Glory (Aden 1980)

A magnificent hosta, though I do not like the way it sometimes sports green leaves. Similar to 'Great Expectations', it has cupped and rugose yellow leaves with blue-green margins. This handsome plant is 30 in. high and 40 in. wide (75 cm by 100 cm) and has white flowers.

'Color Glory', center front

'Crispula', syn. *H. crispula*

One of the first hostas to reach Europe in 1829, it has retained its popularity throughout the years. It has undulate green leaves with white margins, and was one of the earliest white margins to appear. It has white flowers and is 12 in. high and 36 in. wide (30 cm by 90 cm).

Daybreak (Aden 1986)

A stunning deep gold hosta with heavily textured leaves. It grows to about 2 ft. in height and 3 ft. in width (60 cm by 90 cm).

H. 'Decorata', syn. *H. decorata*, 'Thomas Hogg'

Many gardeners know this hosta as 'Thomas Hogg', while others know it as *H. decorata*. Its leathery dark green leaves with their regular white margins are very attractive. In midsummer, purple and sometimes white flowers appear. It is 12 in. high and 18 in. wide (30 cm by 45 cm).

Dew Drop (Walters Gardens 1988)

A very attractive little plant that is 6 in. high and 8 in. wide (15 cm by 20 cm), with white-margined dark green leaves and mauve flowers.

Diamond Tiara (Zils 1985)

I am a great fan of the Tiara group. This particular one has dark green leaves with a neat white margin. It grows 14 in. high and 26 in. wide (35 cm by 65 cm) and has purple flowers. Like its siblings, it rapidly develops into a nice mound.

Dorset Blue (Smith-Aden 1977)

Another splendid selection from the Tardiana group. It has intense blue leaves that are round, cupped and rugose. Small – 8 in. high by 21 in. wide (20 cm by 50 cm) – slow-growing, and thought by some to be the top of the range.

Emerald Tiara (Walters Gardens 1988)

Another little charmer, this time with gold leaves and green margins. It is 14 in. high and 20 in. wide (35 cm by 50 cm), with many purple flowers.

Emily Dickinson (Lachman 1987)

This is a lovely plant with medium-green leaves and a creamy white margin. It has upright leaves and scented lavender flowers. It is 20 in. high and 32 in. wide (50 cm by 80 cm).

Eric Smith (Smith-Archibald 1987)

The hostas in the Tardiana group are all beautiful, small, intense blues, and 'Eric Smith' is said to be the best. It is now being tissue cultured, so it is only a matter of time before it will be available. Grows 8 in. high and 12 in. wide (20 cm by 30 cm).

Fire and Ice

A dramatic hosta, with white leaves surrounded by a bright green border, and lavender flowers. It is 18 in. high and 20 in. wide (45 cm by 50 cm).

Flower Power (Vaughn 1987)

This hosta's large frosted leaves look silvered when they first emerge but gradually turn green. It grows 30 in. high and 46 in. wide (75 cm by 115 cm) and has delightfully scented lavender flowers.

H. fortunei

This hosta is no longer regarded as a species and is a bit of a botanical mystery, since the original plant can no longer be traced. However, there are many selected forms of this hosta available. All are large with excellent foliage.

H. f. 'Albomarginata'

An outstanding landscape hosta, it has green leaves with white margins. These margins sometimes spread over half the blade. The plant is large with mauve flowers. It is 22 in. high and 36 in. wide (55 cm by 90 cm).

H. f. 'Albopicta', syn. H. 'Fortunei Aureomaculata'

The leaves on this hosta emerge a creamy yellow with dark green margins. It is very pretty even though the yellow turns to green later in the season (though you can still see the variegation faintly). It is very popular in Britain because the cool climate allows the variegation stage to stay brighter for longer. I would not be without it. It is 22 in. high and 36 in. wide (55 cm by 90 cm).

Fragrant Blue (Aden 1988)

Not many blue hostas have scented flowers like this one. It's a soft blue and forms a mound 8 in. high and 12 in. wide (20 cm by 30 cm) with white fragrant flowers.

TOP: 'Fragrant Bouquet' ABOVE: 'Francee'

Fragrant Bouquet (Aden 1982)

The soft apple-green leaves of this plant are heart-shaped and wavy with yellow margins. It grows about 18 in. high and 22 in. wide (45 cm by 55 cm) and has large white fragrant flowers.

Francee (Klopping 1986)

One of the most popular of the white-edged green hostas. Neat, tidy and elegant, it grows about 2 ft. high and 3 ft. wide (60 cm by 90 cm). It has lavender flowers.

'Frances Williams'

Frances Williams (Williams 1986)
Controversial and fickle, this hosta is breathtakingly beautiful but does suffer from necrosis, though it is less of a problem in the shade. Deep blue with wide irregular gold margins, its leaves are heavy, heart-shaped and puckered. It has won many awards and was often the darling of the American Hosta Society Popularity Poll. It is 22 in. high and 48 in. wide (55 cm by 120 cm) and has white flowers.

Fringe Benefit (Aden 1986)
An attractive plant that grows rapidly, it has heart-shaped leaves with a cream margin. It is 21 in. high and 36 in. wide (50 cm by 90 cm) and has lavender flowers.

Frosted Jade (Maroushek 1978)
This handsome plant looks frosted and it has a neat white margin with white flowers. It is about 28 in. high and 30 in. wide (70 cm by 75 cm).

Gene's Joy (Aden)
This hosta has pretty cream leaves with a green margin and green streaks to the center. It is albescent, has blue flowers and, like most hostas, needs shade. It grows about 12 in. high and 14 in. wide (30 cm by 35 cm).

Ginko Craig (Craig-Summers 1986)
Popular as an edging plant, this little hosta has flat dark green leaves with a white edge. It grows rapidly and has deep to lighter purple flowers. It is 4 in. high and 10 in. wide (10 cm by 25 cm).

Glory (Savory 1985)
This is a really outstanding gold hosta that holds its color all season. It has heart-shaped leaves, purple flowers and grows about 12 in. high and 24 in. wide (30 cm by 60 cm).

Gold Drop (Anderson 1977)
This pretty little hosta is only 6 in. high and 10 in. wide (15 cm by 25 cm), with white flowers and dull gold leaves that need morning sun to keep the golden color.

Gold Edger (Aden 1978)
An excellent front-of-the-border hosta that increases rapidly. It has yellow viridescent leaves and lots of lavender flowers. It is 8 in. high and 12 in. wide (20 cm by 30 cm).

Golden Medallion
This pretty hosta has golden round, rugose leaves that hold their color and are 6 in. (15 cm) long. White flowers appear in midsummer. It is 14 in. high and 18 in. wide (35 cm by 45 cm).

Golden Prayers (Aden 1976)
The cupped, puckered golden leaves of this hosta are supposed to remind you of upright hands in prayer. It has white to pale lavender flowers and is 12 in. high and 18 in. wide (30 cm by 45 cm).

Golden Scepter (Savory 1983)
This yellow form of 'Golden Tiara' has heart-shaped golden leaves and grows rapidly. It is about 12 in. high and 18 in. wide (30 cm by 45 cm) with purple-striped flowers.

Golden Sculpture (Anderson 1982)

A very large – 24 in. high and 22 in. wide (60 cm by 55 cm) – bright pale gold hosta that is sun tolerant and said to be pest resistant. An excellent plant that is now more commonly available.

Golden Tiara (Savory 1977)

This small, prolific, award-winning hosta (American Hosta Society Nancy Minks Award 1980) is deservedly very popular. With its light green gold-edged leaves it is splendid as an edging plant. It has flowers that are deep purple striped with light purple and that appear in summer. It is 14 in. high and 22 in. wide (35 cm by 55 cm).

Gold Regal (Aden 1970)

A rather large hosta that is 2 ft. high and 2 ft. wide (60 cm by 60 cm), this plant is gold, with stiff, upright leaves and excellent purple flowers.

Gold Standard (Banyai 1976)

This is an excellent medio-variegated hosta that is chartreuse-gold with irregular green margins. It is a perennial favorite and has won the American Hosta Society Eunice Fisher Award (1980) and the Midwest Gold Award (1980). This hosta is about 20 in. high and 36 in. wide (50 cm by 90 cm) and is best grown in some sun; otherwise the gold will turn white later in the season.

Good as Gold (Aden)

Another of my favorites, this hosta is neither green nor gold, but chartreuse. With sun the leaves will turn yellow. It grows 14 in. high and 24 in. wide (35 cm by 60 cm) and has lavender flowers.

Grand Master (Aden 1986)

This is a very good plant, with blue-green leaves and white margins. The leaves are both thick and puckered, while its flowers are lavender. It grows 20 in. high and 20 in. wide (50 cm by 50 cm).

'Great Expectations'

Grand Tiara (Savory 1977)

This useful hosta is a larger version of the popular 'Golden Tiara'. It has oval to heart-shaped green leaves that are edged with a creamy yellow margin. It grows 22 in. high and 34 in. wide (55 cm by 85 cm) and has showy lavender-striped deep purple flowers.

Great Expectations (Bond 1988)

This absolutely splendid plant originated in Britain and has become increasingly popular over the years. It has a light yellow center that is surrounded by wide, irregular margins of blue and green. It is thought by many to be one of the world's most beautiful varieties. It is 22 in. high and 32 in. wide (55 cm by 80 cm).

'Guacamole'   'Hadspen Blue'

Green Fountain (Aden 1979)

Like a green fountain, the leaves of this hosta
cascade from the base and arch over. A very useful
plant, this hosta has lavender flowers and grows
to a large 26 in. high and 36 in. wide (65 cm by
90 cm).

Green Wedge (Klehm)

The very light green frosted leaves of this hosta
are attractive and contrast well with darker
greens. It has white flowers and grows 22 in. high
and 40 in. wide (50 cm by 100 cm).

Ground Master (Aden 1979)

The matte dark green leaves of this hosta have a
wide white margin. Smaller than 'Green Wedge'
(above) at 12 in. high and 20 in. wide (30 cm by
50 cm), the two would blend well together. It
has lots of purple flowers in summer.

Guacamole (Solberg 1994)

This is one of the most beautiful of the medio-
variegated hostas. It has chartreuse leaves outlined
by a wide green margin. Quite large at 2 ft. high and
3 ft. wide (60 cm by 90 cm), it is an outstanding
landscape plant that I would hate to be without.

Hadspen Blue (Smith 1988)

An intense depth of gray-blue leaf color
characterizes this lovely little hosta. It is one
of the wonderful Tardiana group bred by Eric
Smith of Great Britain, and some people think
it is the very best one. The pale lavender to white
flowers appear in summer. It is 8 in. high and
24 in. wide (20 cm by 60 cm).

Hadspen Hawk (Smith 1988)

This is another very desirable small blue bred by Eric Smith. Don't choose one or the other of the Hadspen cultivars: have a little collection. This one has white flowers. It is 8 in. high and 12 in. wide (20 cm by 30 cm).

Hadspen Heron (Smith 1976)

Another small blue by Smith, this time with narrow leaves and white flowers. With its wonderful chalky blue leaves, this hosta has won many awards. It is 8 in. high and 14 in. wide (20 cm by 35 cm).

Halcyon (Smith 1987)

This is one of the most popular blue hostas because of its outstanding heavily textured and glaucous leaves. It has pale lavender flowers. It is 16 in. high and 38 in. wide (40 cm by 95 cm).

Halo (Aden 1976)

This is a pleasant green-leafed hosta with a white margin and lavender flowers. It grows 12 in. high and 16 in. wide (30 cm by 40 cm).

Honeybells (Cumming 1950)

The wonderfully scented white flowers of this hosta nicely complement its pale green leaves. It reaches 26 in. high and 46 in. wide (65 cm by 115 cm) and grows easily and quickly.

Inaho (Japan)

This small hosta is only 6 in. high and 10 in. wide (15 cm by 25 cm). It has purple flowers and narrow yellow leaves that are not margined, but streaked through with green.

Inniswood (Inniswood Gardens 1993)

The leaves on this hosta are gold, heart-shaped, rugose and edged with green. The plant grows 20 in. high and 40 in. wide (50 cm by 100 cm) and has lavender flowers.

Invincible (Aden 1986)

I love the shiny green leaves of this very unusual hosta. It grows about 10 in. high and 14 in. wide (25 cm by 35 cm) and does not mind some sun. The best thing about this hosta is its fragrant lavender flowers.

Iona (Chappell 1988)

The green leaves of this hosta have a gray cast and well-defined, creamy margins. It grows about 10 in. high and 12 in. wide (25 cm by 30 cm) and holds its colors all season. It has lavender flowers.

Irische See (Klose)

The name translates as Irish Sea and it is another beautiful blue from the famous Tardiana group. It is small, only 6 in. high and 10 in. wide (15 cm by 25 cm) and has lavender flowers.

Jade Cascade (Heims)

Another award winner, this hosta is very tall; if grown well it can reach 36 in. in height and 40 in. in width (90 cm by 100 cm). It has pleasant green leaves and makes a wonderful background plant.

June (Neo Plants 1991)

Of all the newer hostas, this is one of the most popular and desirable, with gold leaves bordered by a margin shaded blue and green. It grows about 18 in. high and 30 in. wide (45 cm by 75 cm) and has lavender flowers.

Knockout (Aden 1986)

A very pretty hosta with blue leaves bordered with cream, and lavender flowers. It is 18 in. high and 22 in. wide (45 cm by 55 cm).

Krossa Regal (Krossa)

This plant has a splendid habit that I cannot praise highly enough. It is vase-shaped, graceful and tall at 28 in. high and 60 in. wide (70 cm by 150 cm). In 1988 it was second in the American Hosta Society Popularity Poll, where it still holds a place. It has lavender flowers.

Lady Isobel Barnett (Grenfell)

This very desirable, very large hosta is a sport of the wonderful 'Sum and Substance'. It has green leaves with creamy yellow margins and lavender flowers. It is 30 in. high and 60 in. wide (75 cm by 150 cm).

Lakeside Accolade (Chastain 1988)

Beautiful, very dark green foliage is the main feature of this hosta, which grows about 12 in. high and 18 in. wide (30 cm by 45 cm). It has lavender flowers.

H. lancifolia

This hosta species was one of the first ever to be introduced to the Western botanical world, where it has remained popular as an edging plant. It grows about 12 in. high and 20 in. wide (30 cm by 50 cm) and has narrow green leaves and strong purple flowers.

Lemon Lime (Savory 1977)

The lance-shaped leaves of this hosta are a very pretty pale chartreuse color. It has lavender flowers. It is 12 in. high and 18 in. wide (30 cm by 45 cm).

Little Aurora (Aden 1978)

This hosta is not very big – 8 in. high and 12 in. wide (20 cm by 30 cm) – but it's a beauty, with gold leaves that have a metallic sheen. Its leaves are cupped and puckered, and its flowers are lavender.

Love Pat (Aden 1978)

Any blue as good as this one would be an award winner, and it did, in fact, win the American Hosta Society Midwest Blue Award in 1988. Its deep-toned, glaucous leaves are cupped, puckered and thick. In midsummer, white flowers emerge. It is 20 in. high and 36 in. wide (50 cm by 90 cm).

'Lady Isobel Barnett'

'Loyalist'

Loyalist (Walters Gardens)

You would not think that green and white could look very bright in the garden, but the leaves of this hosta, with dark green edges surrounding wide, clean white centers are very crisp looking. It has lavender flowers. It is 14 in. high and 24 in. wide (35 cm by 60 cm).

Lucy Vitols (Seaver 1989)

I think this is one of the most beautiful of hostas. It has exceptionally heavily textured, puckered leaves of yellow-green, which are encircled by a narrow green margin. It is about 14 in. high and 24 in. wide (35 cm by 60 cm) with lavender flowers.

Maekawa (Aden 1988)

This clone of the species *H. hypoleuca* has strange habits. Its new leaves lie flat on the ground in an exhausted fashion, then later stand up tall. It has white flowers and very large leaves, which have a white coating underneath. It is 18 in. high and 18 in. wide (45 cm by 45 cm).

Maya Gold

This hosta has very attractive light gold foliage and lavender flowers. It grows 22 in. high and 34 in. wide (55 cm by 85 cm).

Midwest Magic

Another attractive medio-variegated hosta with chartreuse-gold leaves that are green-edged and streaked. It grows about 18 in. high and 36 in. wide (45 cm by 90 cm) and has pale lavender flowers.

Mildred Seaver (Vaughn 1981)

An attractive tribute to a well-known American breeder, this hosta makes a nice mound of green leaves with creamy white margins. It grows about 14 in. high and 24 in. wide (35 cm by 60 cm) and has lavender flowers.

Minuteman (Machen)

A dramatic hosta with wide, pure white margins that encircle a green center. A fresh and perky plant, it grows 24 in. high and 42 in. wide (60 cm by 105 cm) and has lavender flowers.

H. montana

Forms of this hosta have been grown in gardens for many years, but it is a bit of a puzzle to botanists because of its variability. From a gardener's point of view it is a wonderfully large-leafed, green hosta that majestically stands 30 in. high and 46 in. wide (75 cm by 115 cm).

'Lucy Vitols'

'Mildred Seaver'

TOP: *Hosta montana 'Aureomarginata'*
MIDDLE: *Hosta nigrescens*
LOWER: *'On Stage'*

H. m. 'Aureomarginata'

This hosta appears early in spring and has huge, pointed leaves that are vividly margined in yellow. It grows to an impressive height of over 3 ft. and is about 5 ft. wide (90 cm by 150 cm). It has lavender flowers.

Moonlight (Banyai 1977)

A well-bred plant that is a sport of 'Gold Standard', this hosta has yellow leaves with a white margin and is particularly useful for lighting up shady places. It grows to 20 in. high and 36 in. wide (50 cm by 90 cm) and has lavender flowers.

Mostly Ghostly

This is what you might call a novelty plant and is really of interest only in the spring. It has pure white, narrow leaves with green streaking, but the plant turns green later in the season. It is 16 in. high and 24 in. wide (40 cm by 60 cm).

Neat and Tidy (Simpers 1980)

This blue-green hosta is well named because it makes an attractive mound that is 16 in. high and 34 in. wide (40 cm by 85 cm). It has white flowers.

Night Before Christmas (Machen 1994)

You will not forget the name of this plant, even if it does seem a bit obscure. It is dramatic and vigorous, and has leaves with white centers that are edged green. It is 16 in. high and 34 in. wide (40 cm by 85 cm) and has lavender flowers.

H. nigrescens

This wonderful hosta is grown mainly in Japan and deserves more exposure in our gardens. The shoots emerge black and the leaves green. In the early part of the season they are frosted an intense ash-gray. It has very tall scapes of white flowers and grows about 24 in. high and 28 in. wide (60 cm by 70 cm).

Northern Halo (Walters Gardens 1984)
This is another green-blue hosta with a white margin and nicely cupped, heart-shaped leaves. It grows 20 in. high and 34 in. wide (50 cm by 85 cm).

On Stage (Aden 1986)
An enormous number of splendid hostas have been bred in the United States by Paul Aden. The leaves of this one have bright yellow centers with irregular green margins. At 14 in. high and 24 in. wide (35 cm by 60 cm), it is one of my very favorites.

Patriot (Machen 1991)
A sport of the mannerly 'Francee', this hosta is a real rebel, with green leaves and a wide, dramatic white margin. It looks remarkably like 'Minuteman'. It is 24 in. high and 42 in. wide (60 cm by 105 cm) and has lavender flowers.

'Patriot'

Paul's Glory (Ruh 1987)
'Gold Standard' has always been a great favorite of mine, so I certainly appreciate 'Paul's Glory', which is not very different. Its leaves have more substance and a more puckered texture; otherwise, at a glance the two plants look very similar. It is 17 in. high and 26 in. wide (45 cm by 65 cm) and has pale lavender flowers.

Piedmont Gold (Stone 1974)
Another award winner (American Hosta Society Eunice Fisher Award 1978, American Hosta Society Midwest Gold Award 1988), this large, robust bright gold hosta is a pleasure to grow. It is 20 in. high and 40 in. wide (50 cm by 100 cm). It has white flowers and likes some shade.

Pizzazz (Aden 1986)
The base of this hosta is frosted blue, and the leaves are heart-shaped and margined creamy white. It is a lovely hosta with lavender flowers. It is 12 in. high and 18 in. wide (30 cm by 45 cm).

H. plantaginea
Hailing from China, this was the first hosta to be grown in Europe. Unlike other hostas, if it is not grown in sun it will not flower, which would be a pity, since the night-blooming flowers have a heavenly fragrance. Its leaves are a fresh green and, because of its need for sun, it is more at home in the perennial border than the shade garden. It is 2 ft. high and 3 ft. wide (60 cm by 90 cm).

***H. p.* 'Aphrodite' (Maekawa)**
This is the double-flowered version of the above species. It has light green leaves and the white flowers have a beautiful perfume. It grows to about 18 in. high and 24 in. wide (45 cm by 60 cm).

Rascal

This hosta is new to me, but I like what I have seen so far. It has vase-shaped chartreuse-colored leaves with green margins – it looks very modern. It is 12 in. high and 18 in. wide (30 cm by 45 cm) and has lavender flowers.

Royal Standard (Wayside Gardens)

This plant has bright apple-green leaves and scented white flowers. It grows vigorously and does not mind some sun. It grows 18 in. high and 36 in. wide (45 cm by 90 cm).

Ryan's Big One (Ryan)

This hosta is so big it looks tropical. It is a fast grower, with huge green leaves and white flowers. It is 30 in. high and 52 in. wide (75 cm by 135 cm).

Sagae (A.H.S. 1987)

This plant used to be called *H. fluctuans* 'Variegated'. It is the darling of the hosta world and tops the American Hosta Society Popularity Poll. Its large frosty blue leaves have a creamy yellow margin. It grows 3 ft. high and 5 ft. wide (90 cm by 150 cm) and has lavender flowers.

Salute (Benedict 1985)

A small beauty with upright, pointed, very blue leaves and lavender flowers. It is popular for its unique upright habit and grows 8 in. high and 12 in. wide (20 cm by 30 cm).

Samurai (Aden)

Many of us would not be able to tell the difference between this plant and 'Aurora Borealis'. Its beautiful blue leaves have wide, irregular yellow margins. The plant needs shade and is said to be not prone to necrosis. Unfortunately, in my experience I have not found this to be true. It grows relatively large, at 24 in. high and 44 in. wide (60 cm by 110 cm).

Sea Dream (Seaver 1984)

This hosta is full of interest, since its heart-shaped leaves emerge a light green color, but quickly turn yellow with a wide white margin. It grows 14 in. high and 30 in. wide (35 cm by 75 cm) and has lavender flowers.

Sea Lotus Leaf (Seaver 1985)

This large blue-green hosta received an American Hosta Society Midwest Blue Award in 1985 for its general excellence. The very rounded leaves are glossy and it has white flowers. It is 20 in. high and 24 in. wide (50 cm by 60 cm).

September Sun (Solberg 1985)

I have a special liking for medio-variegated hostas and this is another of my favorites. Often this type of hosta can be very attention-grabbing, but 'September Sun' is soft and subtle, with yellow leaves margined in dark green and white flowers. It is 22 in. high and 34 in. wide (55 cm by 85 cm).

Shade Fanfare (Aden 1986)

Soft green leaves with a creamy border make this an excellent landscape plant. As its name implies, it does not like much sun. The flowers are lavender. It is 16 in. high and 24 in. wide (40 cm by 60 cm).

Shade Master (Aden 1982)

A lovely gold hosta with white flowers that thrives in a shady place and grows into a dense mound. It is 22 in. high and 38 in. wide (55 cm by 95 cm).

Shining Tot (Aden 1982)

The leaves of this tiny – 2 in. high and 6 in. wide (5 cm by 15 cm) – hosta are heart-shaped, mid to dark green and very glossy. Despite its size, it will grow vigorously given the chance.

H. sieboldiana 'Elegans' (syn. var. elegans)

If any plant is perfect, it has to be this one. It is a large hosta with superb, glaucous gray-blue foliage that is rounded and very puckered. The white flowers sit just over the top of the leaves in summer. It has a majestic presence all its own. It is 3 ft. high and 4 ft. wide (90 cm by 120 cm).

Snow Cap (Aden 1980)

A most attractive plant with blue heart-shaped, puckered leaves with cream margins. It has lavender flowers and is 2 ft. high and 3 ft. wide (60 cm by 90 cm).

Snowden (Smith 1988)

If big is beautiful, then this is a most beautiful hosta. Standing at a majestic 32 in. high and 52 in. wide (80 cm by 135 cm), it has glaucous, rugose leaves that later change to a light grayish-green. It has white flowers.

So Sweet (Aden 1986)

A pretty name for a pretty plant. This one has green leaves with wide white margins. It is 8 in. high and 12 in. wide (20 cm by 30 cm) and gets its name from the fragrant lavender flowers.

'So Sweet'

'Striptease'

'Sum and Substance'

Sparkling Burgundy (Savoy 1982)

A vigorous, upright grower with dark green leaves that are heart-shaped and of heavy substance. It gets its name from its speckled burgundy stems and its burgundy flowers. It is 12 in. high and 20 in. wide (30 cm by 50 cm).

Spearmint

The leaves of this hosta are quite distinctive, with their twisted appearance and heavy yet irregular green margins and cream centers. The striking appearance of this hosta makes it good as a focal point in the garden. It grows 14 in. high and 24 in. wide (35 cm by 60 cm) and has lavender flowers.

Spritzer (Aden 1986)

This hosta is very bright with long yellow floppy leaves and an irregular margin of light and dark green. It makes a splendid accent plant. Its blue flowers appear in summer. It is 18 in. high and 18 in. wide (45 cm by 45 cm).

Striptease (Thompson 1991)

This is a very unusual hosta that is bound to become popular. The leaves have narrow gold centers with dark green margins, and between the gold and the green there is a white strip that gives it its fanciful name. It grows 18 in. high and 24 in. wide (45 cm by 60 cm).

Sugar and Cream (Zils 1984)

This hosta is the white-margined form of 'Honeybells', which is thought to be the better cultivar. It is a personal opinion whether the soft green of 'Honeybells' is less desirable than this white-margined form. 'Sugar and Cream' has sweetly fragrant lavender flowers. It was the winner of the American Hosta Society Savory Award in 1985. It is 26 in. high and 46 in. wide (65 cm by 115 cm).

Sultana (Zumbar 1988)

I love this hosta for its dark green leaves that are edged gold. It grows 7 in. high and 11 in. wide (20 cm by 25 cm). While there are quite a few small hostas of this coloring, this one has real charisma.

'Summer Haze'

Sum and Substance (Aden 1980)

This hosta is splendid. It has won an enormous number of awards (American Hosta Society President's Exhibitor's Trophy 1987; Eunice Fisher Award 1984; Midwest Gold Award 1984; Alex J. Summers Distinguished Merit Hosta 1990), and is an all-time favorite on the American Hosta Society Popularity Poll. It is huge at 30 in. high and 60 in. wide (75 cm by 150 cm) and has golden-chartreuse leaves. It is probably the most popular gold hosta ever. Some sun brings out the gold color and it is said to be pest resistant. It is truly magnificent as either a background or a feature plant.

Summer Fragrance (Vaughn 1983)

The leaves of this hosta are medium green with light and dark green stripes and a cream margin. It grows about 24 in. high and 40 in. wide (60 cm by 100 cm) and has perfumed lavender-purple flowers.

Summer Haze (Barrett)

The very heavy leaves and their deep, glaucous blue color make this 16 in. high and 20 in. wide (40 cm by 50 cm) hosta very pleasing. It is particularly attractive in a container.

Sunny Smiles (Tompkins)

The plant looks rather like 'Shade Fanfare', but the green center is much darker and it has a broad cream margin. It is 2 ft. high and 2 ft. wide (60 cm by 60 cm) and has lavender flowers.

Sun Power (Aden 1986)

This hosta is commonly thought to be one of the very best golds. It has twisted, pointed leaves and an ability to hold its color right through the season. The flowers are pale lavender and it grows 2 ft. high and 3 ft. wide (60 cm by 90 cm).

Super Nova

This is an inverted 'Frances Williams'. The leaves have large golden centers surrounded by wide blue-green margins. They are also deeply cupped and of heavy substance. I do not know if this variety suffers from necrosis. It is 2 ft. high and 3 ft. wide (60 cm by 90 cm) and has white flowers.

H. tardiflora

The glossy dark green leaves are thick and pointed. Mauve flowers appear in summer. It is 10 in. high and 24 in. wide (25 cm by 60 cm).

TOP: Spring growth of 'Tokudama Aureonebulosa'
ABOVE: 'Tokudama'

Tokudama

This beautiful plant was once considered a separate species, but no longer. It is like a smaller version of *H. sieboldiana* 'Elegans'. The leaves are vividly glaucous blue, very heavily cupped and heavily textured. The grayish white flowers appear from early to late summer. The plant is slow growing, eventually reaching 16 in. high and 36 in. wide (40 cm by 90 cm).

Tokudama Aureonebulosa (Maekawa 1987)

If this is not my favorite hosta, it would have to rank in the first half-dozen. It has spectacular cupped leaves, which are a cloudy yellow, margined with a deep blue edge and very heavily textured. It grows to about 14 in. high and 24 in. wide (35 cm by 60 cm) and has white flowers.

Tokudama Flavocircinalis (Maekawa 1987)

Clear primrose-yellow margins border the blue leaves, making this plant similar to 'Frances Williams', only smaller. The leaves of this hosta are puckered and of heavy substance, and the flowers are white. It is 18 in. high and 28 in. wide (45 cm by 70 cm).

Treasure Trove

This hosta has green leaves with a white stripe running around the outside edge. It has a fast growth habit and lavender flowers. It grows about 2 ft. high and 3 ft. wide (60 cm by 90 cm).

Twilight (Van Eiyk)

This hosta is characterized by its dark, glossy green leaves and wide yellow margins. It grows about 18 in. high and 28 in. wide (45 cm by 70 cm). It has lavender flowers.

H. undulata

'Whirlwind'

H. undulata

This clump-forming hosta is the one most commonly used in borders. It has twisted cream leaves with a dark green margin and grows 18 in. high and 20 in. wide (45 cm by 50 cm).

H. u. 'Albomarginata'

This is the green hosta with twisted, white-edged leaves that you see everywhere. What is really interesting about it is that the second crop of leaves is quite different from the first, and often streaked. However, in the spring it will emerge variegated again. It grows 16 in. high and 36 in. wide (40 cm by 90 cm).

Vanilla Cream (Aden 1986)

This little plant kindly changes color over the season. It starts off light green, then turns chartreuse, followed by gold and then finally cream. Four hostas for the price of one! It is 10 in. high and 18 in. wide (25 cm by 45 cm).

H. ventricosa

This species from China and North Korea has broad oval to heart-shaped glossy dark green leaves. Deep purple flowers appear in late summer. It is 20 in. high and 36 in. wide (50 cm by 90 cm).

H. v. 'Aureomaculata'

The leaves of this hosta start out bright yellow with an irregular dark green margin, but the yellow color gradually fades during the summer. It grows 18 in. high and 28 in. wide (45 cm by 70 cm) and has purple-blue flowers.

H. v. 'Aureomarginata'

The large heart-shaped leaves are twisted, with dark green centers and irregular yellow margins. The purple flowers appear in later summer. It is 2 ft. high and 3 ft. wide (60 cm by 90 cm).

Whirlwind (Kulpa 1989)

The leaves on this hosta are upright, twisted and pointed. They have a very dark green margin that enhances the greenish-cream center. Its flowers are lavender. It is 16 in. high and 24 in. wide (40 cm by 60 cm).

'Zounds'

White Christmas (Krossa 1971)
This cultivar is similar to *H. undulata* but the
white centers stay white and have a thin green
margin. It grows to about 18 in. high and 20 in.
wide (45 cm by 50 cm). It has lavender flowers
and makes a very bright-looking clump.

Wide Brim (Aden 1979)
This is a very reliable and good-looking plant. Its
dark green leaves each have a very wide yellow
margin. It grows 22 in. high and 36 in. wide
(55 cm by 90 cm) and has white flowers.

Yellow River (Aden)
The dark green leaves have distinct yellow margins
and form a substantial plant 2 ft. high and 4 ft.
wide (60 cm by 120 cm) with white flowers.

Zounds (Aden 1978)
Metallic gold, heavy-textured, heart-shaped leaves
make this splendid hosta a personal favorite. It is
a hosta that should be more popular. It grows 16
in. high and 30 in. wide (40 cm by 75 cm) and has
white flowers. It is also an award winner.

Bibliography

Aden, Paul (compiler and editor).
   The Hosta Book. Portland:
   Timber Press, 1988.
Grenfell, Diana. *Hosta: The
   Flowering Foliage Plant*. Portland:
   Timber Press, 1991.

The Hosta Journal (American Hosta
   Society).
Schmid, Wolfram George. *The Genus
   Hosta/Giboshi Zoku*. Portland:
   Timber Press, 1992.

Useful Addresses

The importation of live plants and plant materials across borders requires special arrangements, which will be detailed in suppliers' catalogs. Americans must have a permit, obtained through the Web site given below. Every order requires a phytosanitary certificate supplied by the exporter, and purchasers should verify this at the time of order. (If certain plants are exempt from this certificate, the seller will know.) A CITES (Convention on International Trade in Endangered Species of Wild Fauna and Flora) certificate may also be required if the plant is an endangered species.

For more information contact:
USDA-APHIS-PPQ
Permit Unit
4700 River Road, Unit 136
Riverdale, MD 20727-1236
Ph: (301) 734-8645
Fax: (301) 734-5786
www.aphis.usda.gov
Canadians importing plant material must pay a fee and complete an "application for permit to import."

A phytosanitary certificate may also be required.

For more information contact:
Plant Health and Production Division
Canadian Food Inspection Agency
2nd Floor West, Permit Office
59 Camelot Drive
Nepean, ON K1A 0Y9
Ph: (613) 225-2342
Fax: (613) 228-6605
www.inspection.gc.ca

Baldwin Lake Perennials
www.baldwinlakeperennials.com
6110 Baldwin Lake Road
Lino Lakes, MN 55014
Tel: (651) 415-0646
Fax: (651) 415-2749
E-mail: alexejew@usinternet.com

Goldfinch Gardens
www.growingperennials.com
1918 Lenox Road
Jefferson, OH 44047
Tel: (440) 576-0129
Fax: (775) 257-2883

Green Hill Farm Inc.
www.hostahosta.com
P.O. Box 16306
Chapel Hill, NC 27516
Tel: (919) 309-0649
Fax: (919) 383-4533
E-mail: greenhill@mindspring.com

Hickory Mountain Plant Farm
www.hostafarm.com
148 Hadley Mill Road
Pittsboro, NC 27312
Tel: (919) 542-0360

Hostas Online
www.hostasonline.com
208 2nd St. NE
Waukon, IA 52172-1308
Tel: (563) 568-4859
E-mail: bobaxe@sbtek.net

Jim's Hostas
www.jimshostas.com
11676 Robin Hood Drive
Dubuque, IA 52001
Tel: (563) 588-9671
E-mail: jschw94560@aol.com

Klehm's Song Sparrow Perennial
Farm
www.songssparrow.com
13101 E. Rye Road
Avalon, WI 53505
Tel: (800) 553-3715
Fax: (608) 883-2257

Lakeside Acres Hostas
www.gardensights.com/lakeside
8119 Roy Lane
Ooltewah, TN 37363
Tel: (423) 238-4534
E-mail: mc_hosta@bellsouth.net

Naylor Creek Nursery
www.naylorcreek.com
2610 West Valley Road
Chimacum, WA 98325
Tel: (360) 732-4983
E-mail: naylorck@olypen.com

Plant Delights Nursery Inc.
www.plantdelights.com
9241 Sauls Road
Raleigh, NC 27603
Tel: (919) 772-4794
Fax: (919) 662-0370
E-mail: office@plantdelights.com

Singletree Farm
www.singletree.com
P.O. Box 1041
Fletcher, NC 28732
Tel: (828) 654-9415
Fax: (828) 654-9534
E-mail: hostas@singletree.com

White Oak Nursery
www.whiteoaknursery.com
6145 Oak Point Court
Peoria, IL 61614
Tel: (309) 693-1354
Fax: (309) 693-0993
E-mail:
hostas@whiteoaknursery.com

Index

Numbers in bold indicate an illustration.

Index of companion plants for hostas